Critical Acclaim for
Got, Not Got: The A-Z of Lost Footbc

The British
SportsBook 12
Awards

Runner-up, Best Football Book, British Sports Book Awards 2012

"A veritable Dundee cake of a book."
Danny Kelly, talkSport

"Recalling a more innocent time before Sky Sports and millionaire players, *Got, Not Got* is like a long soak in a warm bath of football nostalgia: an A-Z of memorabilia, ephemera and ill-advised haircuts."
In Demand, *Mail on Sunday Live magazine*

"The real magic is the collection and display of the illustrative material of stickers, badges, programme covers, Subbuteo figures and other ephemera. It is astonishingly thorough, well-presented, inspired and indeed had me going, 'yes, got, got, not got, forgot, never seen'."
When Saturday Comes

"A cracking book which whisks you back to a different footballing era."
Brian Reade, Mirror Football

"This memorabilia fest is a delightful reminder of what's gone from the game: 'magic sponges', Subbuteo and, er, magazines for shinpads. Such innocent times, eh?"
FourFourTwo

"The book's great fun. It's an essential if you grew up watching football in the 60s, 70s or 80s. It's a kind of football fan's catnip. Nobody can quite walk past it. They start looking at it and then realise they've got something else they should be doing 10 or 15 minutes later."
Paul Hawksbee, talkSport.

"The best book about football written in the last 20 years."
Bill Borrows, *Esquire*

"A body of work that transcends being 'just a book' by a considerable distance."
In Bed With Maradona blog

"Obviously, everybody over the age of 40 is going to absolutely love this.
There's something for every fan of every club."
Andy Jacobs, talkSport

"Browsable for hours, even days, preferably with your favourite records from the 1970s in the background, this is the Christmas present that every football fan of a certain age yearns to peruse while their neglected partner's busy basting the turkey and getting quietly pickled on cooking sherry… Sit back and be blissfully reminded of adverts, food products, players, toys, kits, magazines, stickers and trends you'd long since confined to your mental attic."
Ian Plenderleith, Stay-at-Home Indie Pop blog

"I've had this for a month but haven't got round to reviewing it because it keeps disappearing. It's the sign of a good book that people repeatedly pick it up and walk away with it. A hardback collection of vintage football memorabilia that you need in your life… It's like finding your old football stickers."
James Brown, SabotageTimes.com

GOT, NOT GOT
The Lost World of Derby County

Derek Hammond & Gary Silke

Pitch Publishing Ltd
A2 Yeoman Gate
Yeoman Way
Durrington
BN13 3QZ

Email: info@pitchpublishing.co.uk
Web: www.pitchpublishing.co.uk

First published by Pitch Publishing 2014
Text © 2014 Derek Hammond and Gary Silke

13-digit ISBN: 9781909626560
Design and typesetting by Olner Pro Sport Media.
Printed in Malta by Gutenberg Press Ltd.

*"I think it was George Clooney who they got
to play me in* The Damned United!
*I told Archie Gemmill that they'd got little
Jackie Wright, the bald man in* The Benny Hill
Show, *to play him!"*

Roger Davies

*"I wouldn't say I was the best manager in the business.
But I was in the top one."*

Brian Clough

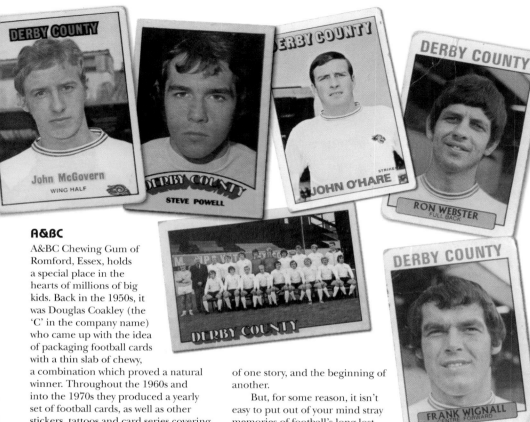

A&BC

A&BC Chewing Gum of Romford, Essex, holds a special place in the hearts of millions of big kids. Back in the 1950s, it was Douglas Coakley (the 'C' in the company name) who came up with the idea of packaging football cards with a thin slab of chewy, a combination which proved a natural winner. Throughout the 1960s and into the 1970s they produced a yearly set of football cards, as well as other stickers, tattoos and card series covering everything from the Beatles to *Star Trek* – and American sports and TV-related cards bound for the US via partner company, Topps.

Nowadays they're worth anything up to two or three quid each for the 1960s and early Seventies cards in excellent condition – though sadly that price drops off steeply for ones with edges chewed and worn, like ours. The 'crinkle-cut' extra photographs given away free with each pack in 1969 are even more desirable, and the little Action Transfers given away as extras in every pack in 1971 are worth anything up to seven or eight quid apiece. This for a small piece of paper which was given away in a packet that cost thruppence.

Unfortunately, in 1974, A&BC lost a long-simmering legal battle and was taken over by Topps-Bazooka. The end of one story, and the beginning of another.

But, for some reason, it isn't easy to put out of your mind stray memories of football's long-lost people and places, the youthful obsessions and outdated rituals that seemed so important back in the day – and, in a strange way, still do. It might be a name on an email that you immediately associate with a recoloured kit on a card, and think: "Not got." Or just a vacant moment when you're whisking down the M1 at 80mph and find yourself wondering… whatever happened to Terry Hennessey?

It isn't everyone who could possibly understand.

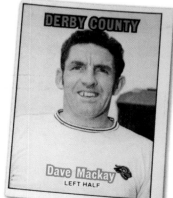

Dave Mac: An off-centre, pink-liveried but still highly sought-after 1970-71 A&BC orange-back!

ACTION MAN

They don't make boys' toys like Action Man any more.

Kids aren't interested in peering through the back of a plastic doll's head and into his 'Eagle Eye' when the maximum thrill available is a slightly blurred view of the back garden. And as for realistic hair and gripping hands... they tend to pall into insignificance next to the Xbox's 3-D virtual world, where it's perfectly possible to drop in on Berlin in 1945 or Pluto in the year 4567, shredding Nazis and aliens alike with a sonic fire ray akin to a red-mist glare from Dave Mackay.

It was bad news when Palitoy didn't include the Rams in the select range of teams they produced team kits for – though the pill could be sweetened if you did like most Derby kids and made do with the near-lookalike Spurs gear.

Because most Action Man enthusiasts kept their figures strictly military, the scarcity value of the football range has more recently seen eBay prices soaring. Complete original 1960s Spurs kits regularly sell on the auction site for silly money, over £300... and would you believe the Action Man team badge given away with the original Tottenham kit pack

Action Man stood stock-still over the ball
in a sorry personification of inaction.

They'd call Action Man un-PC now – an eight-inch multi-skilled terrorist who thought nothing of changing out of his Nazi Stormtrooper uniform into that of a Navy frogman, a Canadian Mountie or an astronaut. And so into his football kit for a kickaround with your sister's Barbie in goal.

Unfortunately, that's when our vicious little accomplice became a complete bore. Whether you had one Action Man or 22, there just wasn't a game you could base around his non-existent ball skills.

The specific types of 'action' mastered by 'the movable fighting man' were limited to bending at the joints and being blown into the air. There was only so much fun you could have dressing a doll in football kit, especially as it exposed his shattered-looking kneecaps. The final straw was the orthopaedic stand which he needed to balance on one leg, hovering over the ball in a sorry personification of inaction.

has sold for an incredible £626. We still have the screenshot from 2004!

If only you'd kept them, Action Man's two-inch-long white socks could now pay for a decent night out.

The Promised Land: Millions of happy hours were spent yearning for hot Action Man gear.

ACTION man OFFICIAL EQUIPMENT MANUAL

A good job done: Now go and stand on a shelf in the Rams shrine for 40 years...

Try painting a microscopic Bass logo over those tricky self-coloured stripes on a bloke who's two inches high.

AIRFIX

Ever since 1955, when they released their 1/72 Spitfire model kit, Airfix had been satisfying little boys' unquenchable thirst for recreating World War II.

You could paint up a boxful of Commandos or Desert Rats and painstakingly put together a Hampden bomber, though how you were supposed to stop the 'cement' from clouding up the glass canopy of the cockpit was anyone's guess.

Even more satisfying than endless war was the 1/32nd scale Airfix Sports Series of Airfix Footballers – your chance to ditch khaki and grey for the far more exciting football colours of black and white, and maybe even a few of those other oppo colours like blue and red and puce.

Up until the mid-Seventies it wasn't too much trouble recreating miniature versions of the kits of the day; but things got a lot trickier after that time.

Go on, you try painting an even row of Umbro sleeve stripes or a microscopic

Bass logo on a bloke who's just over two inches high.

Long boring Sunday afternoons were the perfect time for creating a pair of Umbro or Patrick sock turnovers, until the double misery of *Last of the Summer Wine* and the parental enquiry: "Have you got any homework, son?" reminded you that Monday morning was nearly upon us once again.

Thanks to eBay you can still get that distinctive box through the post with England vs. Germany on the front. Old habits, like old enemies, die hard. And if you've got a steady hand and a couple of hundred hours on your hands, there's no more satisfying way to waste your time.

been assumed to be quite insane, and arrested for causing a breach of the peace. And the same applied to sporting any item of apparel other than a school blazer in a primary colour. Red socks or sky-blue waistcoats, for example, were only ever sported by show-offs, buffoons and variety acts.

So how to let it be known which side you were supporting in the big Cup game on Saturday? That's where rosettes came in: they were the acceptable face of partisanship in more restrained times.

You don't get them any more.

THE ROSETTE

In the olden days, British males over the age of six were only permitted to wear brown, grey, greeny-brown, browny-green or, in moments of extreme flamboyance, navy.

If a chap had worn a football jersey anywhere other than on a football field he might well have

SUN SOCCERCARD No 692

SUN SOCCERCARD No 907

SUN SOCCERCARD No 375

SUN SOCCERCARDS

Allow us to whisk you back to the tail end of the '70s, and one particular night beloved of many football card collectors. The night in question was notable for the long, gruelling, coffee-fuelled marathon undertaken by the anonymous Sun Soccercard artist, chained to his desk with a dozen packs of big bright felt pens and ordered to

S. POWELL (Derby County)

G. RYAN (Derby County)

S. BUCKLEY (Derby Co.)

OCCERCARD No 785

The legendary felt-pen artist
never did get the hang of eyes — or heads.

produce a set of nearly 1,000 player likenesses (or as near as possible).

The results speak for themselves. But just in case you don't recognise your heroes of yesteryear, here's... well, let's just hope their old mums don't recognise them either!

Anything to avoid paying image rights, eh? Even if the man with the felt-pen never did quite get the hang of eyes, their size relative to the human head, and the fact that they're usually pretty much on the same level.

SUN SOCCERCARD No 587

J. DUNCAN

SUN SOCCERCARD No 136

G. DALY (Derby Coun

SUN SOCCERCARD No 444

SUN SOCCERCARD No 116

SUN SOCCERCARD No 80

SUN SOCCERCARD No 576

D. NISH (England)

D. LANGAN (Derby Co.)

R. McFARLAND (England)

G. HILL (England)

Atrocity Exhibition: Starring Roy McFarland as his own granddad and Steve Carter's infamous thoughtful pose.

S. CARTER (Derby County)

11

HINTON HUMMEL SWIVEL BOOTS

As an impressionable child, I witnessed a miraculous vision in the small-ads of a football magazine. A pair of boots so futuristic, so desirable, they just had to be possessed. Not only were the boots in question fashioned from the finest white plastic, they also featured an optimistic gimmick let into their soles, which promised any pre-teen dreamer the ability to turn on a sixpence to devastating effect. Under the ball of the lucky wearer's foot, the studs were set on a rotating turntable.

The ads shouted not about the inevitability of broken ankles, but about NEW REVOLUTIONARY FOOTBALL BOOTS. "Be quicker on the turn with this fantastic new football boot from Hummel."

Not bad for £4.95.

Another contemporary advert makes the scientific point that having studs on a spinning disc could save celeb guinea-pigs Steve Perryman and Alan Hinton loads of energy – as anybody who can recall 'Gladys' dashing down the BBG left wing in his white boots can testify.

"Based as it is on a friction reducing principle," proclaimed Arsenal boss and trained physiotherapist Bertie Mee, "this boot is likely to live up to the claims made for it – fatigue reduction, injury reduction, increased speed on the turn."

They could catch on yet… though whether Alan ever actually wore the Swivel Boots he modelled is somewhat doubtful!

Now swivel on this! Gladys's patent ankle-snappers, in the flesh.

THE CIGARETTE CARD

In the age of No Smoking – when anyone who fancies a tab is forced to stand outside their office in all weathers, and even crowd into a ramshackle lean-to hurriedly added twixt bar and beer garden – it won't be long until kids don't even recognise the reference to a good old-fashioned gasper, already obscured by the slick, sad euphemism of 'candy stick'.

The sweetie cigarette will soon be no more, like the BBG, mud and the sky-high promise of Derek Hales' forty goals per season.

Back in the day, however, they were clearly the best option for L-plate smokers, both in terms of their unique, chalky-sweet flavour and cunning authenticity, courtesy of a dab of pink food colouring on the burning 'hot' end. And they came with a football card, too, if you were lucky – or a fat cricketer or lady tennis player if the dreaded mixed-sports set was in season.

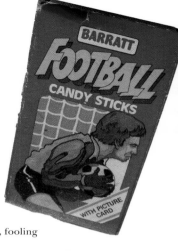

Barratt's and Bassett's packs of sweet cigarettes were a throwback to the cigarette cards that had died out in the war; but we never realised that at the time. We were too busy posing manfully with our sugary cig dangling from our lips, fooling absolutely everybody.

Sweetie cigarette cards are already an obscurity to kids aged under 20 or 30. And the original pre-war mass cult of the cigarette card proper will soon be nothing but a memory clung to by a disappearing breed of oldsters.

No, not the stout men who smoked for England during the war only to be stamped out underfoot in the fallout from NHS cost-cutting exercises determined to make everyone live to 200. But us, the jammy-faced kids who remember the well-thumbed contents of Granddad's hand-me-down baccy tin.

Guess Which Club:
The clue, as Jim Bowen might have said, is in the question.

We posed manfully with a sugary cig dangling from our lips,

fooling absolutely everybody.

GDEN'S CIGARETTES

DERBY COUNTY

PLAYER'S CIGARETTES.

H. THOMS.

UNFORGETTABLES

KEVIN
HECTOR

LOWER-LEAGUE SIGNINGS

Kevin Hector was the Rams' best-ever lower-league signing, costing boss Tim Ward a massive £40,000 in 1966; but Cloughie trumped his predecessor by plucking Roger Davies from non-league Worcester City for just £12K.

"I'd only played about ten games for Worcester," Roger told us. "I remember my debut was against Wimbledon, as they were on their way up. I got a hat-trick in that game, then I got two the next game and then another two. Seven goals in three games was a great start and there was a little bit of paper talk about me.

"Then at training one Thursday night, there's Cloughie walking along the side of the pitch. I didn't think anything of it, I certainly didn't think he'd come to watch me. A week later I got a phone call at work telling me to go along to Derby to see them play Dundee United in the Texaco Cup.

"I went over with my father and met the board and Cloughie after the game. In my first season there they won the championship, obviously the top tier then, and the reserves won the Central League so it was a great time at the club.

"Having played for the reserves I then made my first team debut at the end of that season against Airdrie in the Texaco Cup. A few games into the next season I made my league debut and that was the start of it all…"

15

COMIC COVERS

Have you ever wondered why Derby County play their home games at the Baseball Ground?

Have you ever paused to consider why members of a local county cricket club would end up playing matches on a racecourse?

Have you ever queried the ability of a cartoonist to capture a recognisable likeness of Ol' Big-'Ead?

Have you ever tried to work out what 7/6d would be in modern money, making plans to draw back to Derby a centre-fireworks of the calibre of Steve Bloomer? (It's 37½p, in case your decimal ready reckoner isn't reckoning so readily after 44 years at the back of the kitchen cupboard.)

Or have you ever sought to add together four big numbers… let's say £250,000 + £175,000 + £200,000 + £120,000… in confident expectation of reaching £750,000, only to find yourself £5,000 short?

If so, may we respectfully draw your attention to the oft baffling, always mindblowing wonders of finding your team on a comic cover.

Never again would any random occurrence touch that feeling of being blessed by the gods as when your Saturday morning comic served up a Rams pin-up, a teamgroup or – best of all by several million miles – a cover appearance in *Tiger & Scorcher*.

Like Christmas and birthday rolled into one, it was.

With added curious questions.

Did You Know… anybody who ever won a bloody thing in a Great FREE Competition?

First Division thrills with NIPPER—inside!

EVERY MONDAY

7th September, 1974

Scorcher and SCORE 5p

Did you KNOW…?

Malaysia 60c., Malta 5c.5, Australia 20c., New Zealand 20c., South Africa 20c., Rhodesia 22c.

© IPC Magazines Ltd . 1974

EVERY MONDAY   13th July, 1974

Scorcher and SCORE

5p

SOLVE THE CLUES AND...

SPOT THE TEAM!

THIS WELL-KNOWN CLUB WAS STARTED BY MEMBERS OF A COUNTY CRICKET CLUB IN 1864 AND PLAYED THEIR EARLY GAMES ON THE LOCAL RACECOURSE. THEY WERE FOUNDER-MEMBERS OF THE FOOTBALL LEAGUE IN 1888 AND A FEW YEARS LATER SIGNED A YOUNG FORWARD NAMED STEVE BLOOMER AT A WAGE OF 7/6d A WEEK. HE BECAME THE GREATEST GOALSCORER OF HIS TIME — 291 IN 18 SEASONS IN LEAGUE GAMES FOR THE CLUB AND 28 IN 24 ENGLAND INTERNATIONALS. YET HE ENDED HIS FANTASTIC CAREER ON THE CLUB'S GROUND STAFF!

ALTHOUGH THE "RAMS", AS THEY ARE KNOWN, WON THE F.A. CUP IN 1947 AND TOPPED THE SECOND AND THIRD DIVISIONS, THEY HAVE NEVER SINCE WON THE CUP AND HAD TO WAIT UNTIL 1972 BEFORE TAKING THE LEAGUE CHAMPIONSHIP FOR THE FIRST TIME. BRIAN CLOUGH WAS THE MAN WHO BUILT THAT FINE SIDE, CAPTAINED BY ROY McFARLAND.

BRUCE RIOCH

TODAY'S TEAM INCLUDES FOUR PLAYERS WHO COST THE CLUB THREE-QUARTERS OF A MILLION POUNDS — DAVID NISH (£250,000), BRUCE RIOCH (£200,000), COLIN TODD (£175,000) AND HENRY NEWTON (£120,000). THEIR MANAGER IS DAVE MACKAY, WHO CAPTAINED THE SIDE TO THE CHAMPIONSHIP OF DIVISION 2 IN 1969.

Answer on **GOAL-POST** page...

...nes Ltd., 1974

DENIM JACKET PATCHES

Back in the day, no self-respecting teenager would be seen at a football match or out on the town without a denim jacket rendered almost invisible under the weight of Coffer sew-on patches down the back and arms.

The very sight of these vintage 1970s patches is almost enough to make anybody start nagging their mum to stitch as many as humanly possible on to their parka sleeves and Army Surplus schoolbag.

When we first mentioned our weakness for Coffer paraphernalia to the good men of the Derby County Collection, they sent us a great pile of patches and badges by return of mail.

We were inundated with enough enamel and frayed vintage cotton to weigh down the denim jackets of half the Ozzie End on a blustery afternoon circa 1978. What do kids today do now they can't advertise their love of Northern Soul, Motorhead or Charlie George via their denim jacket? Ah yes, there's always that new-fangled internet.

I'M A DERBY NUT, indeed. DERBY COUNTY TURN ME ON.

How do kids today advertise their love of Northern Soul, Motorhead or Charlie George, Superstar?

Match Winners:
Nowadays, fans have
moved on from cloth
patches to all-over
Rammy tattoos.

DERBY
ARE
DYNAMITE

MIGHTY
RAMS

DERBY COUNTY

GOLD METAL
EMBROIDERED
BADGE

DERBY
COUNTY
RAMS
1ST DIVISION

Levi's

DERBY
ARE A
KNOCKOUT

Cotton is perfectly soft and natural,
alternately warm and cool,
and shrink resistant.

COTTON

It's the sensual associations that come bundled with cotton that make it such a rich source of minor, if largely subconscious, pleasure.

Ahh, the smell of a new cotton T-shirt being pulled on over your head on a Friday night. The slow fade of a favourite shirt, laundered a hundred times by your mum. Cotton next to the skin – warm against the winter cold, cool in summer... the pure smell of plain virginal white, a simple embroidered Ram crest, and no other labels or logos smelling of a modern attempt to cash in.

In 150 years, the only negatives against cotton were an association with hippie cheesecloth and, ah yes, the institutionalised horrors of the slave trade.

Cotton isn't just perfect for clothes because it's easy to take care of and to wash. It's soft because it's made out of perfectly natural fluff. And it's cheap because the fluff grows on trees.

And so some tiresome bean counter inevitably decided to put about the idea that cotton is altogether second rate. Wear it for sports and it apparently now soaks up sweat in a way that you wouldn't want it to be soaked up. Cotton isn't stretchy enough, and it needs ironing, unlike a certain artificial wonder-fabric. They even tried to convince us that shell-suit bottoms were cooler and more comfortable than jeans.

Now, it just so happens that while cotton is cheap, polyester is cheaper. So much cheaper, it's practically free.

Polyester is an artificial plastic made from the acids and alcohol produced when you torch petroleum – in other words, from exhaust fumes.

Polyester is hard-wearing primarily because it's hard. It's rough to the touch, keeps you cold in winter and hot in summer. Wear it in summer, or for sports, and it will make you smell like you've been dead for a week.

Bring back cotton football shirts!

CLUBCALL

Back in the Eighties and Nineties, it was the sheer unavailability of up-to-the-minute club information that made it so tantalising. So valuable.

You wouldn't want everyone else to know that Ted McMinn had a hammy, would you? – not if you were still thinking he might be playing on Saturday. You wouldn't want to miss what 'Wantaway' Dean Saunders had allegedly denied this morning – or boss Arthur Cox's counter-denials of any new ace striker rumours. Ahh, the rumours...

The Clubcall service came as a blessing for all fans – especially those exiled from local news and those trapped at work with the benefit of a free phone to avoid the disgraceful premium call rates.

At the end of the line – literally – was a local newspaper stringer (or at least an Ansafone recording of him) summing up back-page stories from yesterday's evening paper and this morning's tabs. To deliver value for money, he also used to make up juicy filler on the spot, and read it out. S-l-o-w-l-y.

"Hello... and it's a big... Rams... welcome... to your exclusive... front-line... Clubcall service for... Derby County... Football... Club.

"Listen to... Clubcall... for all the latest... news... and... information..."

Because we were paying by the second.

Coining it in: A whole match commentary by phone could cost your company in excess of 200 quid.

DERBY COUNTY

Founded: 1884; Ground: Baseball Ground; Manager: Brian Clough; League Champions: 1972; F.A. Cup: 1946; W
Cup: 1970; Texaco Cup: 1972.

Apply adhesive here only.

Apply adhesi

66

67

68

THE WONDERFUL WORLD OF SOCCER STARS

How many sets of football cards and stickers do you reckon might have been pushed out into the UK market to mark the occasion of the 1966 World Cup?

Ten? Twenty? The answer, you might be surprised to hear, is none. Not a one. Zero.

In recent years a limited test production of A&BC World Cup stamps has emerged, but these are priceless rarities that had no real impact. Even though pocket-size cardboard football cards had been successfully covering the domestic game since the end of the '50s, and European and South American manufacturers had produced trailblazing sticker books for the 1962 finals, it simply didn't occur to anyone to build on these trends.

It was only when England secured Monsieur Rimet's small gold trophy that the enthusiasm really rocketed, kick-starting the British football industry in the

stands, in the shops and in sticker albums up and down the country.

In the second half of the '60s, playgrounds rocked to the tribal rhythm of "Got, got, got, got, not got" as kids flicked through their teetering piles in search of that elusive Peter Daniel, perfectly willing to exchange 200 swaps to fill in the one remaining square left on their checklist.

If us Brits were slow off the mark seeing the possibilities in the market for cards and World Cups, it took even longer to get the ball rolling on the Euro-led non-sticky sticker front.

In 1967, FKS's 'Wonderful World of Soccer Stars' rolled into limited, regional production, reflecting a Golden Age when all you needed to start up business in the football sticker

DERBY COUNTY

Founded: 1884. Ground: Baseball Ground. Manager: Dave Mackay. League Champions: 1972, 1975. F. A. Cup: 1946. Watney Cup: 1970. Texaco Cup: 1972.

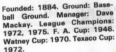

COLIN BOULTON

ROGER DAVIES

ARCHIE GEMMILL

CHARLIE GEORGE

KEVIN HECTOR

LEIGHTON JAMES

22

JOHN ROBSON   ARTHUR STEWART   RON WEBSTER   FRANK WIGNALL

14

Founded: 1884. Ground: Baseball Ground.
Manager: Dave Mackay. League Champions:
1972, 1975. F.A. Cup: 1946. Watney Cup: 1970.
Texaco Cup: 1972.

PETER DANIEL   ROGER DAVIES

market was a picture deal with an agency – no worries if the images were a season or two out of date, that's what retouching brushes are for – and a distribution deal around the corner shops of Britain.

The idea took off, and 1968 saw the first widely available sticker set, largely repeating the previous year's mugshot efforts. The following season's largely accidental mix of action shots and head-and-shoulders upped the excitement greatly and has rarely been bettered, still offering a real window into the Wonderful, and sadly Lost World of Football in the Sixties.

The business model was clear. Give any football-mad child a packet of (not really very accurately titled) stickers, an album and a pot of Gloy gum, let him stick his first sticker into the allotted slot, surrounded by another dozen blank spaces taunting him, and let nature take its course...

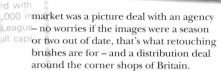

ER STARS
77-78

JUBILEE OFFER 10p

DERBY COUNTY

Founded: 1884
Ground: Baseball Ground
Manager: Brian Clough
League Champions: Nil; F.A. Cup:
1946; Watney Cup: 1970

Derby County FC

COLIN BOULTON

PETER DANIEL

ARCHIE GEMMILL

LES GREEN

KEVIN HECTOR   TER

LA

ALAN HINTON   McFARLAND

JOHN McGOVERN

23

FANZINES

Following on from the Seventies' music-led revolutions in DIY publishing, it took a while for football to catch up, but eventually fans took to their cranky old typewriters, hunting and pecking and ker-chinging out their frustrations, and learning all-new reprographic skills along the way.

They were tired of hearing 'The Fans' View' expressed second hand in the media, where the final word, the final edit, was always predictably happy and safe. Before the 1980s, every word written about football came from an industry perspective – tapped out by writers who were paid by newspapers, magazines, television companies or club programmes, which were in turn reliant on the FA, the League or the clubs themselves.

It's a tough job, running the back page of a local paper without access to news information, player interviews or pictures.

No such problem for the first wave of fanzine rebels, who offered an all-new diet of uncensored opinion cut with terrace humour, finally putting the majority view of 20,000 regulars above the handful of professionals and hired hands – the chairman, the players, the manager, the gentlemen of the press box – who were just passing through.

Suddenly your familiar old programme seller had a bit of competition on the streets from titles such as *Hey Big Spender, C-Stander* and *The Sheep*.

No matter if they were presented under headlines written using felt-pen, Letraset or John Bull Printing Outfit No. 7: here, for the very first time in print, were negative as well as positive views on our beloved clubs and teams, jokes at our own expense, better jokes at our unmentionable local rivals' expense, album and gig reviews, stories of away trips, pubs and pies... always pies.

And, somewhere along the way, we discovered it wasn't just the fans in our corner of our ground who felt the same way about all-seater stadiums and ID cards, about the wreckers who came to football to chuck bananas and seats on the pitch, and the wreckers who came bearing calculators. And pies.

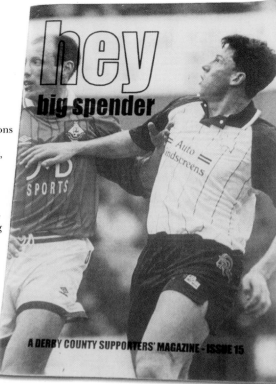

A DERBY COUNTY SUPPORTERS' MAGAZINE - ISSUE 15

Publish and be damned: not every club welcomed the attentions of their very own, devoted fanzine...

GREAT MOMENTS IN HISTORY

According to this essential old-school learning aid – a veritable encyclopedia in handy Roladex card-file format, with thousands of facts in small print on the reverse – there was the Big Bang, then there were Romans and Vikings, and then Brian Clough and Peter Taylor were signed up to make history at Derby.

Admittedly, we might be missing one or two of the less eventful cards due to pocket-money shortages over the stretch of the series, available in 782 weekly parts. But that's the gist of world history.

Crikey, these cards were like the entire internet printed out in handily portable form for commentators of social or football bent. Essential reading, then and now!

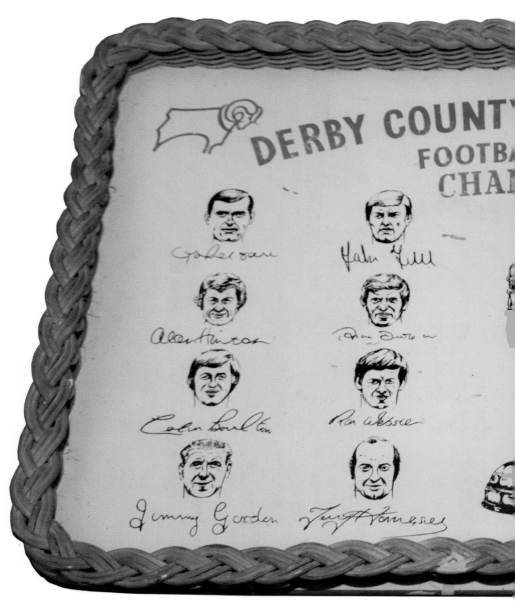

TEA FOR TWO

Fresh off an episode of the *Antiques Roadshow* filmed in the vintage-friendly environs of drizzly Buxton, here's a family heirloom recently adjudged by resident experts to be quite literally priceless.

"It was the ancient tea stains and cake crumbs that did the trick," opined renowned domestic historian Angela Rippon, "as much as the quality rustic woven-plastic edging and the superb Old Master caricatures of the championship winners back in the day."

Even after the passage of aeons, there's little or no doubt which star player each cartoon represents.

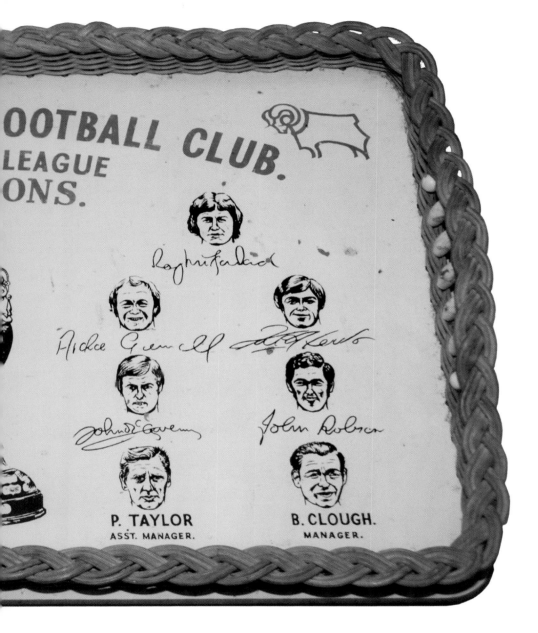

OOTBALL CLUB.
LEAGUE
ONS.

Roy...

Alan Gemmill

...Kerr

John O'Govern

John Robson

P. TAYLOR
ASST. MANAGER.

B. CLOUGH.
MANAGER.

"To be fair," chipped in silverware specialist Hugh Scully, "the exclusive addition of their original personal autographs help in the identification process as well as adding several noughts to the value of the superb antique tea tray."

The proud owners of the tray,

Mr and Mrs Maxwell of Belper, were thrilled by the valuation, summarised by Michael Aspel as "for insurance purposes, practically beyond value. If only Clough and Taylor had been invited to scrawl on it, it might have been worth a bob or two!"

Football League Review

THE OFFICIAL JOURNAL OF THE FOOTBALL LEAGUE

ONE SHILL

THE FOOTBALL LEAGUE REVIEW

Run from the back bedroom of secretary Alan Hardaker's Blackpool bungalow, the Football League was devoted to showing everyone what a big, happy family their 92-member club was. The *Football League Review* was a feelgood customer mag, given away free inside club programmes, where it bolstered many four- or eight-page lower-league efforts. The *FLR* was conspicuous in its absence from several larger League grounds, where power brokers were already wary of growing League influence.

Super Kevin Hector, League championship trophy... and lairy matching tie and tank-top set from Woolies.

However, in stark comparison to the petty politicking backstabbing golf-clubbing small-minded scrap-metal merchant football-club owners of the 1970s, fans dug the freebies to bits – especially if Kevin Hector featured on the cover.

The *Review* was 5 pence 'when bought separately'; which is to say never. It was full of behind-the-scenes peeks at the day-to-day running of all the League clubs, an article on the bootroom at Barrow being just as likely as a visit to the Arsenal trophy room. Then and now, its allure was almost entirely down to staff photographer Peter Robinson, who spent whole seasons travelling around snapping mascots at Mansfield and tea-ladies in Tranmere, thinking up ever more unusual formations for his teamgroups.

"I was conscious that I was different when I talked with other photographers at games," he told *When Saturday*

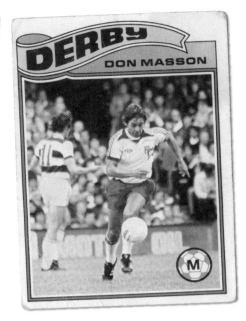

The Review was 5 pence 'when bought separately'; which is to say never.

Comes. Robinson never missed an angle, an expression, an oddity or a location, showing more interest in football culture than the game itself. "I felt that you didn't just have to start photographing when the ref blew his whistle. I was interested in the whole build-up to the game."

HASTILY RECOLOURED KIT

Although there was a lot less movement in the transfer market than today, the photo agencies that supplied the football card and sticker manufacturers in the Sixties and Seventies were rarely bang up-to-date.

Cue the burning of midnight oil as heads were snipped off and reapplied to new team-mates' bodies, and old shirts hastily penned with new colours. Or, in the peculiar case of QPR's Don Masson, a huge childish Ram and flyaway gull-wing collars.

You've got to love bodge jobs like this FKS sticker of Rod Thomas of Swindon Town sneakily updated with a felt pen to suggest he's not wearing red and white.

FKS albums even carried a straight-faced 'guarantee': 'In order to maintain authenticity, some of the players have been photographed in clothing which is not necessarily their official club colours'.

Rod Thomas:
Not in Swindon. Honest, Guv.

ITV SUNDAY AFTERNOON FOOTBALL

Today an old friend emailed me an mp3 file entitled 'Star'.

I instantly recognised the blaring, barely-in-control brass section of the *Star Soccer* theme tune and was transported back to a mid-Seventies Sunday afternoon at two o'clock.

The Sunday dinner that had taken Mum hours to cook was wolfed down in two minutes. Roast beef and Yorkshire puddings lay in my stomach, barely chewed, as I rushed to turn on the old black-and-white telly so that it would warm up in time for that blasting fanfare, played over a backdrop of one of the Midlands grounds,

Remember the theme tune **from ATV's *Star Soccer?***

and the welcoming South Midland baritone of commentator Hugh Johns – a dark-chestnut, favourite-uncle tone underscored with a hint of Naval-issue cigarettes.

There was little room for manoeuvre in the editing suite, back then. The main game, however incident-packed or dull, ran for fifteen minutes up to a half-

Afternoon Delight: Roast beef, Yorkshire pud and good old Hugh Johns.

time ad break, followed by another quarter of an hour for the second half.

Part three brought fifteen minutes of a game from another ITV region. Granada's Gerald Sinstadt was the voice of *Kick Off;* Tyne Tees was Kenneth Wolstenholme on *Shoot*, while LWT's *The Big Match* was fronted by Brian Moore...

After part four's brief highlights of another game – usually Norwich or Ipswich from Anglia's *Match of the Week* with Gerry Harrison – and a round-up of results, the weekend seemed almost over.

Dozens of games went untelevised every weekend between 1969 and 1983 and that's why seeing your team was so special. With perhaps only two or three TV appearances in a lean year, the novelty never wore off.

No. 0024

DUPLICATE

The Derby County Football Club, p.l.c.

CAPITAL, £2,000,000, DIVIDED INTO 1,080,000 ORDINARY SHARES OF £1 EACH AND 920,000 2½% NON-VOTING PREFERENCE SHARES OF £1 EACH

This is to Certify that _____ MR. I. R. MAXWELL

of _____ HEADINGTON HILL HALL, HEADINGTON, OXFORD _____ is the Proprietor

of _____ 25 _____ Ordinary Shares, fully paid, numbered _____ 1104594 _____ to _____ 1104618 _____ inclusive in

'The Derby County Football Club Public Limited Company,'

subject to The Memorandum and Articles of Association and the Regula_____ said Company,

Given under the Common Seal of the Company,

this _____ Twenty Sixth _____ day of _____ July _____ 19 91

DIRECTORS

Secretary

No Transfer of the above-mentioned Shares will be registered without the production of this Certificate

CHANCER CHAIRMEN

In the late 1980s, perhaps the most amusing of the new breed of chancer chairmen was Michael Knighton – a Derbyshire property trader domiciled in the Isle of Man, with a frustrated yearning to play keepy-uppy in front of the Stretford End with a new Man U scarf over a big suit and tie. It wasn't long before the chancer had installed himself as chairman-manager at Carlisle United and led the club into administration.

Cripes, the story of our Michael makes the arrival of Robert Maxwell at Derby seem like a breath of fresh air – a multi-billionaire businessman bringing his all-round expertise and sensibilities to the challenging role of chancer

chairman. As such, the club goes down as one of the first in Britain to facilitate a genuine Bond villain's interest in the game of football.

It's enough to make you yearn for the lesser evils of the old-school chairman, a more parochial class of self-made man who had run every football club for the past 100 years. A pillar of the local community, Mr Chairman doled out jobs for life in his palatial nut-and-bolt factory in the middle of town, drove a Jag with a carphone and had the Football League in his shiny waistcoat pocket. Bring him back!?!

As honest as the day was long: Ján Ludvík Hyman Binyamin Hoch.

FOOTBALL CLUB

MR. ROBERT MAXWELL
CHAIRMAN

31

LEAGUE LADDERS

Wahey! Rams top of the League!

But there was more to your youthful flights of League Ladder-related fantasy than mere self-centred feelgood relish. There was also the bottom of Scottish League Division Two to consider (or maybe, if you were feeling generous, the bottom of the fourth division, and the basement trapdoor beckoning into non-League Hell). That's where a good old English emotion known as *schadenfreude* took over – and where you found Forest among a cluster of lesser clubs such as Dirty Leeds, Chelsea and Liverpool. Not to mention every other side that had put one over on County in the past three seasons.

Gifted to us in the build-up to the season's big kick-off by *Shoot!* or *Roy of the Rovers* or one of the old-school shoot-'em-up comics such as *Lion* or

Ground:
The Baseball Ground,
Derby.

Team tab:
Cut out and keep,
and collect the
whole set of 92!

Valiant, the empty league ladders came first, closely followed over a number of weeks with the small cardboard team tabs designed to be slotted into their ever-changing slot in the scheme of things.

In the days before computers, even before Teletext, the appeal of being able to stare at the league table was considerable. But, after the third or fourth week, updating your league ladders became a bit too much like hard work.

And that's when you could see what it would look like if East Fife were somehow suddenly transported to second in the League behind its natural eternal leaders. Ha! Swansea in the First Division, and Burnley in the Fourth! And all those lesser Midlands clubs mysteriously close to going out of business – pointless, crowdless and hopeless, as God intended.

f the new s

SHOO

HOO

SHOOT!

FREE LEAGUE LADDERS

Exciting Exclusive Features

1st DIVISION

English League

CCER WEEK

70

3rd DIVISION | 4th DIVISION

VISION

the pre-v
Th
cons
livin
offer

and
ALL
and
by th
powe
As it

For
the B
figure
Th
bare
show
high

the a
matcl
added
petitic
total
THE
31,7

Know all there to know with SHO
week SHOOT ill be packed with informative
about every st of the
aphs and pin-ups
teams.

Last
the p

obby Styles
in Training full colour,
Story of the ropean Cup,
Moore w e first of a

in in
33,09

SHOOT/G

	1st DIVISION		2nd DIV
1	DERBY	1	
2	ARSENAL	2	
3	QUEEN'S P.R.	3	
4	LIVERPOOL	4	
5	IPSWICH	5	
6	MANCHESTER U.	6	
7	WEST HAM	7	
8	EVERTON	8	
9	MANCHESTER C.	9	
10	STOKE	10	
11	LEICESTER	11	
12	NEWCASTLE	12	
13	LEEDS	13	
14	NORWICH	14	
15	BIRMINGHAM	15	
16	SUNDERLAND	16	
17	MIDDLESBRO'	17	
18	WOLVES	18	
19	TOTTENHAM	19	
20	WEST BROM	20	
21	COVENTRY	21	
22	ASTON VILLA	22	

DERS

H LEAGUE

2nd DIV

1	ST. JOHNSTONE
2	E. STIRLING
3	MORTON
4	HAMILTON A.
5	STRANRAER
6	ARBROATH
7	ALBION R.
8	COWDENBEATH
9	ALLOA
10	STIRLING A.
11	EAST FIFE
12	DUMBARTON
13	AYR U.
14	QUEEN'S PARK
15	MONTROSE

PROGRESS CHART..

	1976								
Position	AUG	SEP	OCT	NOV	DEC	JAN	FEB		

33

STRIKE!

We asked Roger Davies if he recalled when Clough and chairman Sam Longson locked horns, and Clough left.

The players were considering going on strike – which must have included you?

"Yes, I was a part of those meetings," Roger admitted, "when it was seriously discussed."

So what turned things around?

"Probably the FA telling us that we risked getting *sine die* suspensions if we refused to play! Cloughie wanted to whisk us all away to Spain to get out of the way. Terry Hennessey was our Union rep at the time, talking to the FA. So we decided that we had to play, and then Cloughie turned up at the game and went and sat up in the stand.

"The club were quite clever bringing Dave Mackay in. Probably about 80% of the players had played with Dave when he was at the Baseball Ground before. Probably the only first team players who hadn't played in the championship-winning side with him were myself and John O'Hare.

"Dave was honest enough from day one, he said if anyone doesn't want to be here then come and see me. He was great to play for, in a different way from Cloughie, and the club were vindicated when we won the League title in 1975."

Life after Brian Clough

Meet the new boss, NOT the same as the old boss.

FUMES

Smell: it's the rogue sense, running out of control. At times, your nose can seem almost randomly wired up to your memory. Smells can just creep up on you.

It doesn't matter where I am when I catch a whiff of pipe smoke – I might be in a pub garden or in the street, walking behind a devil-may-care pensioner – and instantly I'm ten again. I'm sitting wrapped up at the football with my dad and Uncle Ken and someone we only ever knew as The Shiverer, and there's an old boy a couple of rows in front of us, struggling to spark up his half-time shag.

It's as if I'm actually there, transported in time by this magic smoky smell. I can actually see and feel and hear, although the Tannoy system is still largely incomprehensible. I can see the muddy pitch, the slanted stand roofs and factory chimneys.

It might be the same for you and the smell of red-hot metal fumes drifting over the ground from Francis Ley's fabrication plant next door.

It takes a million-to-one chemical combination to unlock a memory.

You can't just expect to march in and press the right buttons with Chanel No. 5; Brut 33; a dozen red roses. The smells that really do the trick are less predictable than that. Like Playdoh – that sweet strawberry plastic smell, quite distinct from ordinary plasticine warming up on the radiator.

It can't be long before someone starts marketing the bottled essence of what it smells like to be a kid.

'Aromatherapy', they could call it... take a sniff back in time from a little pot of damp school corridor varnish; or the sparking static smell of a nylon jumper being pulled over your head. Smoke. Or hot metal castings.

Free beer and topless barmaids: Bring back the smoky boozer and ashtray carpets, eh?

DROP IN FOR A DRINK

DUTCH COURAGE

The merest suggestion of a bottle of beer is now enough to send the club dietician into a dead faint, but it wasn't always so.

Brian Clough seemed to subscribe to the theory that it was better for any player to be drunk and relaxed rather than sober and nervous.

Of course, in order to protect the reputation of certain Rams legends of the Sixties and Seventies, we'd never suggest that anyone took to the BBG pitch post-nip or post-sherbet, let alone under orders from the top.

However, we have no such qualms about revealing the controversial tactics of Clough and Taylor once they'd shifted camp into Tricky territory over the M1.

Sensing some 'nerves' as his Forest side travelled up to Liverpool for a 1978 European Cup tie, Cloughie ordered the coach driver to stop at a pub. After this unscheduled lunchtime session came a relaxing afternoon in the hotel before getting the 0-0 draw they needed at Anfield.

Later that season Clough carried out another experiment, unconventionally opting for Champagne before the League Cup Final against Southampton. He ordered his team into a private room at their hotel, locked the door and told them no one was leaving until all the bubbly was history – preferring his players

to be hung over at the breakfast table rather than lying awake worrying.

The end was nigh at Derby, during the infamous 'resignation' incident, when chairman Sam Longson actually had the grille pulled down on the club bar to stop Clough and Taylor further inspiring themselves with free drinks.

But still we're not allowed to report that alcohol is a performance-enhancing wonder drug. Or that it might be worth the current Rams regime giving it a shot – no pun intended!

MIRRORCARDS

Back in the sunny 1971/72 season, the *Daily Mirror* was kind enough to give away a set of football cards featuring teamgroups of all 92 League clubs, plus the four Home International squads. The cards could be collected up and stuck on a large wallchart entitled 'Bobby Moore's Gallery of Soccer Sides'.

As if that weren't enough, it was then possible to order from the newspaper's HQ a special giant-size 'My Club' card to take pride of place in the middle of the poster.

Not many punters made it this far down the line – the Rams 'My Club' card is one of the rarest around

To be frank, few punters made it this far down the line – making the Derby County 'My Club' card (not to mention that of some of the smaller third and fourth division teams) one of the rarest around. Especially in mint condition, as those that were ordered were almost inevitably slapped straight on to Junior's wall!

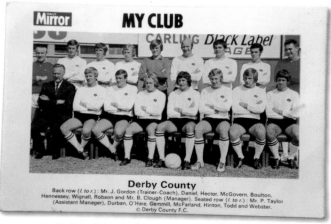

Derby County

Back row (l. to r.): Mr. J. Gordon (Trainer-Coach), Daniel, Hector, McGovern, Boulton, Hennessey, Wignall, Robson and Mr. B. Clough (Manager). Seated row (l. to r.): Mr. P. Taylor (Assistant Manager), Durban, O'Hare, Gemmill, McFarland, Hinton, Todd and Webster.
© Derby County F.C.

The *Father Ted* perspective challenge: the small card is big and the big card is far away.

STAR SO

SERIES O

Buy the

regularly

your serie

MIRRORCARD

Back row (*l. to r.*) : Mr. J. Gordon (Trainer-Coach), Daniel, Hector, McGovern, Boulton, Hennessey, Wignall, Robson and Mr. B. Clough (Manager). Seated row (*l. to r.*) : P. Taylor (Assistant Manager), Durban, O'Hare, Gemmill, McFarland, Hinton, Todd and Webster.
© *DERBY COUNTY F.C.*

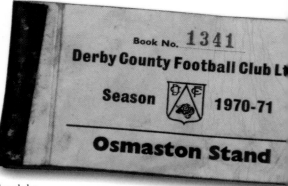

TICKETS (WHEN TICKETS WAS TICKETS)

Nowadays a ticket is nothing but a computer printout. That's if you're lucky enough get a ticket at all.

All too often nowadays, the clubs save time and money by issuing impersonal plastic credit cards for season-ticket holders to trigger the turnstile. Which means season-ticket holders aren't exactly season-ticket holders any more, doesn't it? It saves on printer ink and postage, it's furiously futuristic and sensible and saves trees and probably the planet… but what we really want is a nice old dog-eared piece of paper to stick in an album. Or better still, the lovely hollow shell of a season ticket that you'd carried around in your pocket for the best part of a year – quite possibly in a custom leather slipcase so

A ticket, yesterday: Complete with idyllic, if optimistic, family scene.

your trousers weren't soiled by the rub of common paper.

Oh to drop by the ticket office on match day, when a dithery old bloke wearing a rubber thimble would thumb you a pristine ticket from his neat pile, ripping it free with a practised fold and tug. He'd ask you where you'd like to sit, and write in the seat number by hand.

TACKLING FROM BEHIND

There would appear to be some confusion regarding the tackle from behind, and whether or not it has been outlawed. In 2005, FIFA removed the phrase "from behind" from the laws of the game, replacing it with "a tackle which endangers the safety of an opponent," which was to be "sanctioned as serious foul play."

With this change, it seemed that uncompromising defenders and combative midfielders would immediately have 180 degrees restored to their field of operations, but sadly that isn't the way things have panned out.

Because the tackle from behind is a challenge you don't see coming – that would only spoil the surprise – there's no chance, no time to get your feet off the ground, which means an increased chance of injury. And this applies even if the defender does manage to get a toe-end to the ball a millisecond before he sends you twelve feet in the air.

Referees continue to interpret any tackle from behind as 'endangering safety'. In fact, they continue to interpret any tackle as 'endangering safety'.

And so gone forever is the sort of 'Welcome to the Baseball Ground' incident – what many of us in these parts prefer to think of as a 'Welcome to Elland Road' incident – that used to give half the crowd such an enjoyable chance to get on their high horse, and the other half an opportunity to ask "What?" and shake their heads in such righteous confusion that they almost convinced themselves it was genuine.

The tackle from behind is a challenge you don't see coming.
That would only spoil the surprise.

Hey, Terry!
We reckon it will definitely take a stud.

MUD

Mud used to be as central to the game of football as the ball itself. Placed on a freshly repainted centre-spot. By the Man in the Middle. At Central Park, Cowdenbeath...

Mud was synonymous with football, a crucial factor in its tactics, skills and disciplines. We played in mud and paid to watch better players struggle to overcome mud – their control, balance and ability to dive and tackle like demons all dependent on mud.

From the terraces, football smelled
of mud. On big occasions, we sneaked
on to the pitch and helped ourselves to
hallowed clumps of mud.

Best of all, on Saturday morning, we
picked the dried, inverted mudprint out
of our studs – a perfect, stud-holed fossil
record of last weekend's 6-0 defeat –
tossed it on the changing-room floor and
started all over again, temporarily clean
and full of hope for what the mud might
bring.

43

PANINI

Panini's first set of domestic League cards came out under the Top Sellers name in 1972, but it wasn't until later in the '70s that they hit their stride, producing uniform, trusted sticker sets which were actually sticky.

Under this onslaught, A&BC lost their way and were bought out by the American firm Topps, who temporarily brought a little baseball card razamatazz and glam-rock style to proceedings. Still, the days of cardboard were numbered – as were those of good old FKS, who responded to the Panini steamroller with their own sticky set of bizarre gold stickers in 1978 before quietly biting the dust.

The Panini Revolution stood for reliability, professionalism, mass popularity and a return to hundreds of near-identical head shots, albeit with little flags and team crests.

It seemed that everyone had a copy of that debut Football 78 album in their school bag, along with a pile of swaps held in place with a laggy band. Our new favourite thing was twice as hefty as its predecessor, weighing in at a fat 64 pages; each club spread over two pages instead of one, and in total there were 525 stickers to collect.

The stickers themselves were beautifully designed, clear head-and-shoulders shots with a club badge and a St George or St Andrews flag because, yes, the Scots had been included too. Clydebank's Billy McColl got to have his own sticker, and the English Second Division was also covered with a team group and badge for each previously ignored team.

Ah, those badges. There was a heartbeat jump when you ripped open your packet and saw a gold foil County badge nestling among the half-dozen stickers...

Panini reigned for a good fifteen years, never straying far from their '78 blueprint, producing a series of highly

Dave 'David' Langan: When footballers didn't generally insist on using their full first name.

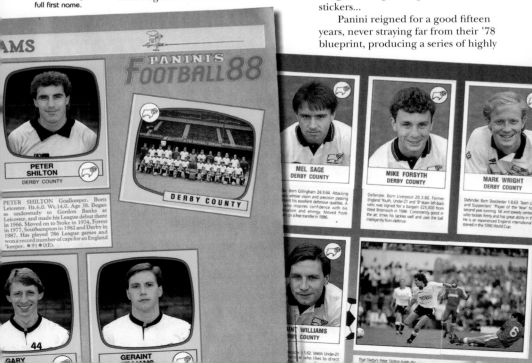

JOHN MIDDLETON

collectable and well-loved albums until they, in turn, were replaced by Merlin around the time the Premier League was launched and the licensing fees leapt up.

The Panini Football 1991 sticker album proudly bore the crests of the Football League and the PFA together with that of the Scottish League and pro body counterparts. What Panini didn't know was that Merlin (AKA good old Topps, if you read the small print) were waiting in the wings to scupper the comfy status quo with a deal already tied up with the brand-new Premier League.

In 1992, Panini's remaining PFA licence allowed them only to produce stickers of the players

rather than any club details. How sad it was to see official stats replaced by weedy 'captain's comments' and it got worse when kits were no longer able to be shown – players trotted out in standard white PFA boiler suits – or else players' kit recoloured in lairy greens, reds and oranges in the utterly emasculated 'Super Players From Top Teams' of '96.

While Panini responded by skittering down the leagues for material, Merlin's Premier League 1994 debut featured PL badges, team groups, full info and players in kits, bright and beautiful. There was even a page for Sky TV cards.

John Middleton: Part-exchange in the Archie Gemmill Forest deal. But the Rams ended up with Shilts!

STEVE POWELL

FOOTBALL LEAGUE
FIRST DIVISION

DERBY COUNTY

Derby County

The Baseball Ground

Chairman: G. Hardy
Manager: Tommy Docherty
Secretary: A.S. Webb
Coach: Frank Blunstone
Captain: Roy McFarland
Year formed: 1884
Ground capacity: 38,500
Record attendance: 41,826 v Tottenham, Division 1, September 1969
Honours: Division One Champions: 1971-72, 1974-75.
Division Two Champions: 1911-12, 1914-15, 1968-69.
Division Three (North) Champions: 1956-57.
FA Cup winners: 1945-46.
Colours: White shirts, dark blue shorts, white stockings.
Change colours: Blue & white striped shirts, white shorts, blue stockings.

DERBY COUNTY

TOMMY

Born in Gl
career wit
came youth
he played
last four y
full caps
managemen
also mana
Park Range
Portugal. M
team for a
to take over
the Second
the FA Cup
up in 1975,
tember 1977

COLIN BO

Goalkeeper
Ht. 5.11. W
League deb
ing started
cadet. Has be
1971, and a
casions.

DERBY COUNTY
TOMMY DOCHERTY (Manager)

DERBY COUNTY
COLIN BOULTON

DERBY COUNTY
ROD THOMAS

ROD THO
Defender.
ft. 1. W

THE CHAMPIONS

DERBY COUNTY

(... to Right) D. Anderson (Asst. Manager), K. Hector, J. McGovern (now Nottm. Forest), J. O'Hare (now Nottm. Forest), R. Webster, C. Boulton, G. Mosley, P. Daniel, S. Powell, C. Todd, J. Gordon (Trainer, now Nottm. Forest). A. Hinton, J. Bourne, D. Nish, A. Gemmill, D. Mackay (Manager), R. McFarland, R. Davies, B. Rioch, R. Thomas, H. Newton. Inset: F. Lee.

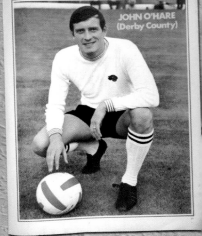

JOHN O'HARE
(Derby County)

N HINTON Derby County

THE BEDROOM SHRINE

You can rebuild it, y'know – the bedroom shrine of your youth when you loved them all, even the dodgy old full-back on whom the adults would pour scorn and derision.

From a time when you wanted to see their images last thing at night and first thing in the morning; arranged in teamgroup ranks, watching over you while you slept.

The thrill of opening a *Goal*, or *Shoot!* or *Tiger* and seeing a real actual Rams star featured on a colour poster – or, even better, a team photo in the centre spread – might not be so keen now. But don't let that hold you back.

You can still get the horrible woodchip wallpaper we all had in our bedrooms, and paint it that turquoise light blue that was in vogue in the mid-Seventies. Someone will still have the recipe.

And there are people on eBay who make it their business to go through old magazines and annuals pulling out the posters of your club, flogging them by the dozen. The collection that took you seven years to accrue can now be obtained in a couple of days.

It won't have organically spread across your wall over the years like a fungus of devotion, but it will still look magnificent.

Almost certainly, the wife will understand.

SHOOT!GOAL   ROGER DAVIES
Derby

Terry
Hennessey

DAVID NISH Derby County

46

COLIN TODD

KEVIN HECTOR
Derby

BRUCE
RIOCH
Derby

HENRY NEWTON
Derby

SHOOT/GO

DERBY COUNTY

FRANCIS LEE
Derby County

SHOOT/GOAL

DERBY
WINNERS

47

THE AUTOGRAPH BOOK

Gone out of existence. Withdrawn from the field. Abandoned. Missed. Passed by.

Everything we come across on this journey through the Lost World of Derby County is no more. They thought it was all over – and they were dead right.

The autograph book was unlike any other of its day. Its cartridge-paper pages were blank, devoid of words and lines, with the built-in compensation of alternate pastel shades – chalky blue, green, pink, yellow. The outer corners of the pages were missing, rounded off so as

PLAYERS AND OFFICIALS ONLY an hour after the match. The players are missing, too: men who didn't need a minder at their side to talk to a twelve-year-old about the afternoon's brawls and cannonballs. The kind of players whose personally signed message you'd want to treasure forever. Leighton James. Bruce Rioch. Tony Macken…

The warning signs came when first two, then three, and now four of the five attackers in every team were phased out, goalscoring deemed surplus to

The kind of players whose message you'd want to treasure forever.

Leighton James. Bruce Rioch. Tony Macken…

not to offend the hand of an honoured victim. The spine of the leather-bound booklet ran down the short side, so it lolled open invitingly. On the cover of the book there was no author's name or title, just a single, golden word in a curly typeface. And then there was the vital loop of elastic to hold the book closed in the owner's back pocket, either encircling the whole precious volume, or just stretching over a single corner.

Lost. Let slip. No longer in our possession.

It isn't just the autograph book that has bitten the dust in recent years, but also the crowd of small boys hanging around the locked double door marked

requirement. Local heroes fell out of fashion. Red-faced stoppers failed to evolve with changing times, and so soon became extinct. And the best player in so many teams of the Sixties and Seventies became the first called up to the great kickaround in the sky.

All gone, but not forgotten.

Then as now, football magazines and club shops churned out sheets of pre-printed (quite literally auto-) autographs to help save the all-important stars time and hassle. It's all a question of supply and demand, see? But it's odd how much more charming the old sheets seem in comparison to today's handily pre-signed official postcards.

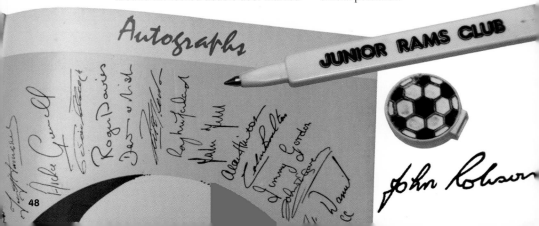

48

BAB

The BAB Souvenir Company was known for just two, instantly recognisable products:

1 – The lairy, you might say imaginatively, coloured football club crest sticker

2 – The star-player sticker, always carefully labelled in case of any doubt as to who was depicted.

The modern-day attraction to collectors is essentially down to the fact that, in the early Seventies, hundreds of thousands of children simply couldn't resist unpeeling backs of the stickers and attaching them to their school bags, school desks, bedroom walls and younger siblings, testing to the limit the proud boast on the retail cards:

"GREAT! Collect ALL these football 'club' badges," shouted the old counter box. "Sticks to almost any surface."

Children simply couldn't resist
sticking the stickers on their school bags,
school desks, bedroom walls
and younger siblings.

It could almost have been a long-term strategy to boost values to collectors.

And then there's the sloppy way the company continually recycled their few sticker designs in new and unlikely colours, with endless minor variations, which appeals to the obsessive modern collector.

Admittedly, we mainly like them because they're funny. Is that the least flattering image of Alan Durban you ever did see? Terry H is doing his best to stifle a snigger.

SUBBUTEO

Subbuteo was by far the most popular table-top representation of football, and its '00'-scale figures still hold a special place in the hearts of blokes across the globe. Part of the game's appeal was due to the huge range of accessories which, while unnecessary for the actual playing of the game, did prop up an illusion of realism and 'add to the big-match atmosphere'.

Plastic pitches were one of the ugliest developments in Eighties football. QPR, Luton and Oldham became unbeatable at home because they mastered the art of playing on a surface that had all the properties of lino – sliding tackles were out, except for players wearing motorcycle leathers under their shorts. Meanwhile,

good old Subbuteo exhibited their usual dogged determination to keep up with the times, producing their own 'Astroturf' pitch – although, if their 'grass' pitch was made of green baize cloth, and the 'Astroturf' surface from slightly different baize cloth, it's unclear in what sense it was any more 'artificial'.

The rampant hooliganism of the time puts into stark perspective any complaints about plastic pitches, leading as it did to football attendances going down and spike-topped fences going up. Subbuteo didn't shirk its remit to mirroring the game and replaced its friendly green picket fences with prison railings and mounted police to keep any potential plastic yobboes off the pitch.

The 'Heavyweight' figures of the Seventies had a stance that suggested they were well up for it.

Heavyweight champ: This Rams-specific figure with his XL hand-painted collar is a real rarity.

The actual Subbuteo playing figures of the late Sixties to late Seventies are known these days as Heavyweights, with their National Service haircuts and a stance that suggested they were well up for it.

The Seventies also saw short-lived and unloved 'Scarecrows' and 'Zombies' figures before the Eighties brought the more detailed, and more popular, 'Lightweights' which endured to the mid Nineties.

Although accessories such as the dugouts and the ambulance men, the TV tower with mini-Motty, the floodlights

4   5   6

14

29

44

59

and VIP figures (including Queenie handing over a tiny FA Cup) were affordable and always welcome on a Christmas morning, the ultimate prize had to be the Subbuteo stadium, complete with a decent crowd of ready-painted spectators. Unfortunately, they were beyond the pocket of most kids' parents and you'd count yourself lucky to have a single, foot-long stand with a couple of dozen spectators dotted around it.

We used to buy packs of unpainted spectators – fifty per box, all as naked as the day they were moulded – and only after weeks of eye-damaging work on Polo-Neck Man, Fatty, Celebrating Man and his equally Celebrating Girlfriend, did we discover the ultimate irony: with stands on all four sides it was virtually impossible to play the game without nudging a stand and causing a mini-stadium disaster.

Oh, come on, let's go up the park and play football.

Squelch

SQUELCHERS

When it comes to 1970s petrol freebies, many fans of a certain age have their nostalgic favourites. It might be the miniature plastic player busts issued by Cleveland Petroleum in 1971, or the foil club badges that were given away every time dad bought four gallons of Esso 4-star. But it takes a special kind of purist to reserve a missionary zeal for the delights of Esso's set of Squelchers.

These were small, badly bound booklets full of facts of varying degrees of likelihood (and veracity, as it turns out), designed "to squelch arguments about football." Though of course, in pubs and playgrounds all over the country, all they really did was start arguments...

"Squelch!" you were supposed to butt into other people's conversations, fumbling open your blue plastic folder to recite: "Derby assistant manager Peter Taylor

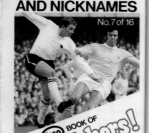

CLUB COLOURS AND NICKNAMES

No. 7 of 16

AN Esso BOOK OF Squelchers!

was a goalkeeper at Middlesbrough at the same time Brian Clough was a record-breaking striker and England international!"

There were 16 themed Squelchers in the set. And, even today, it's hard to do without them on a long away trip by rail.

"Don't be silly," you're invited to read aloud as a conversation-starter. "Derby County's Baseball Ground is so called because it was opened as an actual baseball ground in 1890, for workers at Francis Ley's foundry!"

Woe betide any fan who should ever make a factual blunder within your earshot. The chance of a lifetime! An opportunity to whip out your Squelcher and humble a fellow football fan.

"Anyone can score a goal from a penalty"

Squelch! It's Terry Hennessey, having extracting his boots from that thick BBG mud.

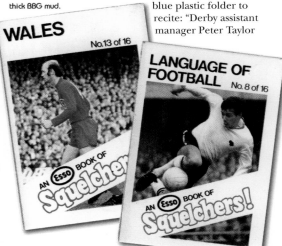

WALES No. 13 of 16

AN Esso BOOK OF Squelchers!

LANGUAGE OF FOOTBALL No. 8 of 16

AN Esso BOOK OF Squelchers!

"SQUELCH!

Frank Wignall boasts a record England scoring ratio with two goals in two international games!"

"SQUELCH!" you announce to your brand-new acquaintance in the snug at the notorious Twirling Star. "Derby County were on the end of the worst ever Cup Final defeat back in 1903 when a series of mishaps at the Crystal Palace stadium resulted in a 6-0 defeat to mighty Bury."

Surely a fitting way to draw to a close any further discussion regarding the finest ever football giveaways. With an all-time classic collectable. And before anyone gets hurt.

COUNTY

TEAMS THAT YOU CAN RECITE

When teams were teams rather than private contractors of fleeting acquaintance, the first-choice line-up would go unchanged for seasons on end, with the boss blooding a kid or adding perhaps one new face over the close season, but only to replace the arthritic right-back who had just enjoyed his testimonial year.

You knew your team was a team because they piled into a team bath after the match, rather than wearing flip-flops and initialled dressing-gowns and insisting on private shower cubicles. You knew they were a team because their surnames seemed to rhyme when you recited them.

Wallington, Blades, Buckley, Williams... What's the Rams side you can automatically recite?

Boulton, Webster, Robson, Hennessey, McFarland, Mackay, McGovern, Wignall, O'Hare, Hector, Gemmill, Durban.

What's the Rams team you can automatically recite?

Every year, you'd hear a news story about a fan who had named their firstborn after their whole beloved team.

Take a bow, Colin Ronald John Terence Roy David John Frank John Kevin Archibald Alan Blenkinsop. You'll be coming up 44, next birthday. And, of course, it's now a family tradition to name a little one after your heroes, even though it doesn't really work so well in the era of 40-strong Premier-era squads.

So spare a thought for poor little Lee Craig Craig Shaun Richard Paul Jeffrey Christopher Martin Jamie Johnny Lee John Mark Ben Kieron Conor Will Mason Valentin Callum Michael Mats Jake Adam Zak James Simon Andre George Patrick Kelle Blenkinsop.

'LoveLee' for short. Smashing little girl.

53

The A-Z scoreboard could often prove a distraction for players who liked a flutter on the fixed odds...

HALF-TIME SCOREBOARD

Not long ago, while at a match, I was checking on the scores of our fellow promotion contenders on Livescore.com. It was taking a little longer to download than usual (probably about eight-tenths of a second) and I was poking the screen of my iPhone in an exasperated fashion.

And then I thought: "Whoa there!

Whoa there, old son... when did we get so impatient?"

A few short years back, before we carried around the collective knowledge of the world in the palm of our hand, we had to wait until half-time to see how the other games were going. Then they'd be viewed on the electronic scoreboard, accompanied

by boos or cheers, as appropriate.

Travelling even further back through the mists of time to the late Sixties (which now appears technologically equidistant between the Saxons and Samsung) most grounds employed a simple but effective code which allowed supporters to see the scores around other grounds. It involved a chap with a wooden box full of metal plates with numbers on them, arranging them next to a row of letters, usually situated on the front wall of a stand. In the days when a programme cost a shilling, everybody bought one, and you turned to the appropriate page to crack the code.

And, somehow, we got by.

Testimonial Brochure

THE TESTIMONIAL MATCH

When was the last time you went along to pay your respects to a great old servant of your club, putting up with the prospect of a meaningless friendly against big local rivals – it's never quite the same, on their days off – in order to chip in to the loyal clubman's retirement nest egg as he looked forward to living in temporarily reduced circumstances and having to get a proper job? Eh?

There's no such thing as a testimonial match any more. Lining the pockets of a multi-millionaire with the proceeds of a kickaround against a team with the suffix 'XI' doesn't count. The vital elements of long service, need, mutual gratitude and respect are all absent.

Long service, need, mutual gratitude and respect...

Colin Boulton: Fourteen years at the BBG... and an almost casual ability to fly.

Roy McFarland Testimonial Trust   Souvenir Programme 20p

DERBY COUNTY v F.C. BRUGES

Baseball Ground Derby Wednesday 9 November 1977 kick-off 7.30

HENRY NEWTON BENEFIT
COMMITTEE Presents
Derby County versus Nottingham Forest
at the Baseball Ground Derby on Monday April 3rd 1978 kick-off 7.30

SOUVENIR PROGRAMME 20p

Colin Boulton testimonial brochure 20p

Derby

Roy McFarland

International Appearances	28
International Goals	0
League Appearances	393
League Goals	39
Height	5'11½"

Southampton

Charlie George

...national Goals	0
International Appearances	1
League Goals	63
League Appearances	231
Height	5'11"

1982 DATA plus
CLUB CHANGES

BRITISH
STARS SET 1

FREE *pack offer inside!*

TOP TRUMPS

Kids used to flip their cards at playground walls, either trying to get closest to the bricks or cover the oppo, and of course we jammed millions of pounds' worth of cards into the spokes of our bikes to get a groovily authentic engine noise.

Hence, Top Trumps were invented in the '70s to give card-owning a little more of a competitive dynamic:

"My Roy McFarland trumps your Archie Gemmill 8 to 3 in the 'Heading' stakes."

"Gah, if only you'd gone for 'Midfield Tenacity' – the Gemmill is yours."

This head-to-head game-playing tradition was revived in the mid-'90s by Subbuteo Squads sets, and powers into the future with Shootout cards.

Don't bother trying to take on Chris Martin in the 'Heavy Metal CD Collection' category, but remember he's beatable by Will Hughes in the 'Future Barcelona Star' stakes.

Derby

Don Masson

International Appearances	13
International Goals	5
League Appearances	445
League Goals	104
Height	5'8"

Beat that: Don trumps Charlie in every category except 'Luxuriance of bubble-perm'.

WE ALL SCREAM FOR ICE CREAM

We're guessing the ice cream industry hasn't had a great time of it recently, given the drizzly nature of our rather rubbish summers (notlikewhenwewerekids). Well, maybe they should start giving football badges away with their ice cream, like they did in 1971. That would soon have us running to the end of the street every time we heard the chimes playing 'The Whistler and his Dog'.

Mister Softee issued their '1st Division Football League Club Badges'

for the 1971/72 season, featuring the 22 top-flight clubs plus England and Wales... but not Scotland where, presumably, it's a bit chilly for ice-cream and lollies.

Rarer editions of this set, which was issued for one more season, were branded 'Lord Neilson' and 'Tonibell'.

Was it just our dads that said: "You know when the chimes are going? That means they've run out of ice cream"?

"Y'know when the chimes are going?

That means they've run out of ice-cream."

THE TURNSTILE

"Enter through the narrow gate. The gate that leads to damnation is wide, the road is clear, and many choose to travel it. But how narrow is the gate that leads to life, how rough the road, and how few there are that find it..." – Matthew 7:13-14

Clunk-kerlunk-clunk-clunk: how satisfying it was to push against a heavy, old-style wrought-iron turnstile, and feel that little surge of relief and anticipation that it used to trigger every time: "I'm in..."

In through the Gates of Heaven – or maybe Hell.

The first game I ever went to, there was a wink and a nod and I was lifted over, while the turnstile man pocketed a little extra for himself, thus rendering all official attendance records useless.

Forty years later, steel bars form a wall-to-ceiling barrier and my season ticket beeps into an impersonal, incorruptible machine, turning a little light green.

The old Rush Preventative Turnstiles were built to last forever by the likes of WT Ellison & Co Ltd, Engineers of Salford, and only when the stands of our childhood began to be demolished and they were isolated, blinking in the light, did we realise quite what beautiful pieces of engineering they were. This one's in Andy Mac's back garden, and features in the *Telegraph* approximately every other week!

Clunk, click: Last year, Rams nut Andy Mac shelled out over £700 to walk up his own driveway.

59

Chicken in a basket, gym teacher, Raquel Welch and Benny Hill.

FOCUS ON...

Back in 1974, cheeky scouser Roy McFarland lay to shame every modern footballer who ever filled in a programme questionnaire name dropping property portfolios and £750 cocktails.

He couldn't remember his birth date, but he knew who he'd most like to meet: that Raquel Welch in a sauna bath, presumably after taking her for a spin in his Triumph Stag and treating her to some roast lamb. It wouldn't be a long journey though, that would be a drag.

He didn't like being knocked out of the European Cup by Juventus, but he did love Frank Sinatra, golf and going to West Germany.

And John Prescott McGovern tells it like it is. Or rather was. **CAR:** Ford Escort Mexico. **FAVOURITE TV SHOW:** Deputy Dawg. **FAVOURITE SINGERS:** The Rolling Stones. John hated losing, but take him to Holland and give him some scampi and then show him a John Wayne movie and he'd be a very happy man... **MISCELLANEOUS LIKES:** Champagne, tennis, presumably not at the same time.

Meanwhile Aldershot-born Scotsman Bruce David Rioch was finding it difficult to leave his previous club, Aston Villa, behind...

FOCUS ON

ROY McFARLAND
DERBY & ENGLAND

NAME: Roy McFarland
PLACE: Liverpool
DATE: I can't remember!

CLUB: Tranmere Rovers

Nose
Slag

OTHER TEAM: Liverpool
DIFFICULT OPPONENT: Jim

MEMORABLE MATCH: Beating
up in 1972

DISAPPOINTMENT: Being
out of the 1972-73 European
Semi-Finals by Juventus

BEST COUNTRY VISITED: West
Germany
FAVOURITE FOOD: Roast Lamb
MISCELLANEOUS LIKES: Playing golf
any game
FAVOURITE T.V. SHOWS: Plays, Top
of the Pops
FAVOURITE SINGERS: Frank Sinatra,
Tamla Motown music
FAVOURITE ACTOR/ACTRESS: Paul
Newman, Natalie Wood
BEST FRIEND: John Wignall, now
playing in Australian football
BIGGEST INFLUENCES ON CAREER:
Being under Brian Clough and Peter
Taylor for six and a half years, and
playing with characters like Dave
Mackay, Willie Carlin and Terry
Hennessey

PREVIOUS CLUBS: Luton, Aston Villa.
FAVOURITE OTHER TEAM: Aston Villa.
MOST MEMORABLE MATCH: The 1971 League Cup Final at Wembley Aston Villa v Spurs.
BIGGEST THRILL: Playing in the above match.
BIGGEST DISAPPOINTMENT: Not reaching the First Division in five years with Villa.
BEST FRIENDS: Former Aston Villa team mates Brian Tiler and Ray Graydon.
BIGGEST INFLUENCES ON CAREER: Vic Crowe and Ron Wylie at Villa.
Bruce, mate, you've got to let it go...

FOCUS ON

JOHN McGOVERN
DERBY COUNTY

FULL NAME: John Prescott McGovern
BIRTHPLACE: Montrose, Scotland
BIRTHDATE: October 28th, 1949
HEIGHT: 5ft 8ins
WEIGHT: 10st 5lb
PREVIOUS CLUB: Hartlepool
MARRIED: No
CAR: Ford Escort Mexico
FAVOURITE PLAYER: Jimmy Greaves
FAVOURITE OTHER TEAM: Liverpool
MOST DIFFICULT OPPONENT: Johnny
Giles
MOST MEMORABLE MATCH: Last season's
European Cup-tie against Benfica at the
Baseball Ground

BIGGEST THRILL: Winning the
Championship in 1972
BIGGEST DISAPPOINTMENT: Being
knocked out of the European Cup in the
Semi-Finals by Juventus
BEST COUNTRY VISITED: Holland
FAVOURITE FOOD: Scampi
MISCELLANEOUS LIKES: Champagne,
tennis
MISCELLANEOUS DISLIKES: Losing
FAVOURITE T.V. SHOWS: Deputy Dawg,
Cinema, Old Grey Whistle Test
FAVOURITE SINGERS: Rolling Stones
FAVOURITE ACTORS/ACTRESS: John
Wayne, Malcolm McDowell, Raquel Welch

BEST FRIEND: I have many
BIGGEST INFLUENCE ON CAREER: Brian
Clough
BIGGEST DRAG IN SOCCER: Injuries
INTERNATIONAL HONOURS: Scotland
Under-23 caps
PERSONAL AMBITION: To stay in the First
Division for ten years
PROFESSIONAL AMBITION: As above
IF YOU WEREN'T A FOOTBALLER
WHAT DO YOU THINK YOU'D BE? A tennis
player
WHICH PERSON IN THE

61

THE 'RAMS'
FOR THE TEXACO CUP

FIDDLING WITH THE RULES

It wasn't just Jimmy Hill on *Match of the Day* who was always pressing madcap plans for an offside zone, bigger goals and three points for a win. In the 1970s, every Tom, Dick and Harry had a Big Idea how to bring back goals into the game now that winning, and shutting up shop, was becoming increasingly important.

Two points for a win... plus a bonus point if you scored three goals!

Watney-Mann, those noted brewers of fizzy beer, came up with a wizard wheeze to set the game back on fire, and decided to showcase their ad-men's action plan in a special pre-season tournament. Featuring the two top-goalscoring teams from each of the four divisions, the 'action-packed' Watney Cup set off the 1970/71 season "dedicated to setting a fast pace, giving lots of action and providing more goals."

Fulham-Derby was the first game of what proved a hugely influential tournament, though not because the 'no draws' rule brought about extra time and a 3-5 final result – this was Britain's first ever corporate-sponsored football trophy. Out on the pitch, the inaugural Watney Cup was also notable for the first ever shoot-out in the British game (with Denis Law becoming the first ever player to miss).

Meanwhile, the Texaco Cup kicked off in the same season, featuring seemingly random clubs from England, Scotland and the Irish Republic. It was chiefly of interest because the FA allowed the offside rule to be amended, with a no-offside line painted across the pitch 25 yards from goal. Also, a bonus point was awarded (in addition to the standard two for a win, one for a draw and zilch for a defeat) to any team that scored three or more goals in a match.

Not to be outdone, the Watney Cup was back again the following season with offside only in force inside the penalty area. The final ended 4-4 between West Brom and Colchester, and then 4-3 on penalties to the sharp-shooting Baggies.

Apparently, the experiment created too many goals, too much fun for the FA bigwigs:

ONE OF TH
TI NGS THAT EV
TO SOC

THE
WATNE
CUP

Good lu
The W

WATNEY CUP 1971
JULY 31st - AUGUST 7th

IT'S WATNEYS' RULE ABOUT NO DRAWS!*

*The penalty system of deciding drawn games was first introduced in the Watney Cup 19—

the Watney Cup was scrapped after 1973, and the games played are sometimes even excluded from players' and clubs' records because of the sacrilegious rule fiddling.

Nevertheless, the Watney Cup still warrants a spot in the Rams' trophy cabinet at Pride Park (while Chesterfield are eternal holders of the Texaco Cup!)

The two tin cups throw up a weird pattern in the career of Clough and Taylor who, apart from lifting the Second Division trophy in 1969 and the League championship trophy in '72, also picked up the somewhat less auspicious Watney and Texaco Cups in '71 and '72.

When they took over at the Trees, it's Quite Interesting to note that the Dynamic Duo won not just the odd

first-class European pot, but also the apparently semi-fictional European Super-Cup. Not to mention the Anglo-Scottish Cup 1977; the Mercantile Credit Trophy 1988; the Simod Cup 1989 and the Zenith Data Systems Cup 1992!

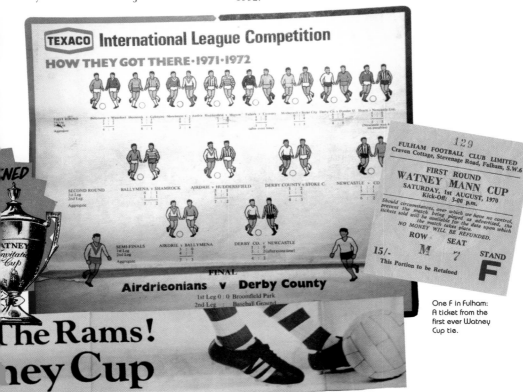

TEXACO International League Competition

HOW THEY GOT THERE·1971·1972

FINAL
Airdrieonians v Derby County
1st Leg 0 : 0 Broomfield Park
2nd Leg : Baseball Ground

One F in Fulham: A ticket from the first ever Watney Cup tie.

129
FULHAM FOOTBALL CLUB LIMITED
Craven Cottage, Stevenage Road, Fulham, S.W.6
FIRST ROUND
WATNEY MANN CUP
SATURDAY, 1st AUGUST, 1970
Kick-Off: 3·00 p.m.

ROW M SEAT 7 STAND F
15/-
This Portion to be Retained

The Rams!
ney Cup

PAINTING THE PENALTY SPOT

"I played at Derby in the '70s when mudbaths really were mudbaths," boasts ex-Rams striker Derek Hales. "A lot of the time there was so much sand on that pitch it was like Margate beach. I was in the stand in April 1977 when Gerry Daly was about to take a penalty and the pitch was so muddy and sandy that the groundsman had to come on and paint the penalty spot."

Match of the Day's John Motson remembers ref John Yates pacing out the 12 yards with groundsman Bob Smith to repaint the spot "lost in two or three inches of mud."

The Rams were already 3-0 up and won the match to avoid relegation!

"Gerroff me whitewash!"
Rams groundsman plots painting new pen spot eight yards out...

KIRKLAND CLOUGH X

BRING BACK CLOUGHIE!

Do you remember this? Whatever happened to that? Bring back the other! To anyone who isn't up to their neck in British football, it might seem we're all obsessed with the distant past. But that isn't an accusation anyone could aim at the Derby County faithful back in 1973, when fans and players worked together in a rare pincer movement, desperately attempting to turn back the clock just a matter of days.

Events were set in motion when Brian Clough and his assistant Peter Taylor sensationally resigned their positions following the Rams' 1-0 away win against Manchester United. The idea was a grand double-bluff, forcing a power struggle designed to dislodge director Jack Kirkland and chairman Sam Longson, who resented his protégé's growing media celebrity.

MANAGER

Real actual:
The door sign from Cloughie's BBG office, signed by the man himself.

The object of their concern, almost inevitably, was Brian Clough – the manager who had led the club to the Second Division championship, then the First Division title and the semi-final of the European Cup.

To illustrate the episode, here's a couple of evocative items of ephemera, once so common that they were handed out in their thousands, or even possible to pick up for free – but which have now become relatively scarce some 40 years later.

For the first piece of treasure, thanks go out to Andy 'Relics of the Rams' Ellis, who kindly sent in what he calls "an interesting sticker used in the 'Bring Back Clough and Taylor' campaign in October 1973".

To Leicester Players And Fans.

Welcome. Have A Good Day. May The Better Team Win.

To Derby Fans. The Chant is —

Clough In - Board Out

Cloughie Shoots For You Now You Shoot For Him We Will Win !!

Don Sha
Bill Hol

Plese Supply
Please Pass On.

Clough himself called it
"the worst decision I ever made..."

While the players went on lightning strike, fans produced a snowstorm of stickers, posters and leaflets (remember banda sheets? Whatever happened to banda sheets? Bring back banda sheets!) in support of the 'Bring Back Cloughie and Taylor' campaign.

But with Longson revelling in his re-emergence as top dog, there was no going back on what Clough called "the worst decision I ever made" – now not just the stuff of legend, but fiction and film, too.

Harking back to happier times at the Baseball Ground, thanks are due to Andy Mac for this historic black-and-white flyer which was given away inside the *Football League Review* (itself a free Football League publication given away inside club programmes) back in 1969.

Well done indeed, Mr Clough...

Congratulations to
Brian Clough

MANAGER OF DERBY COUNTY F.C.

on his nomination by the

panel of 20 leading

British Sportswriters

as

FOOTBALL MANAGER
OF THE MONTH

(ENGLAND)

AUGUST 1969

SHOOT!

Allowed one comic a week, I'd already graduated from the entry-level *Beano* to *Scorcher*, but not until the summer of 1974, while immersed in the West Germany World Cup, did I consider myself man enough to step up to *Shoot!*

Eight pence was the price of admission, and I was soon in beyond the full-colour cover of Billy Bremner playing for Scotland against Brazil.

Now I could dive headlong into an article by Bobby Moore – every week, he'd let us backstage, behind the scenes in the life of a living, breathing football hero – and what's more I could puzzle over the fiendish problems posed in 'You Are the Ref'; study up-close World Cup action featuring Australia, Scotland, Holland, Zaire, DDR and Yugoslavia; chortle at the 'Football Funnies'; 'Focus On' Paul Gilchrist of Southampton (Miscellaneous Likes: motor racing, oil painting, music), and realise there were people just like me all over the country, courtesy of the 'Goal Lines' letters page and 'Ask the Expert' readers' queries.

If I was lucky, there'd be a full-page star poster to add to my shrine, though this only happened once in a blue moon. It's difficult to explain now how a photo could be so prized, Blu-Tacked instantly up on your wall, but in the days of black newsprint papers and monochrome TV, the eight colour pages in *Shoot!* were like oases in a grey desert.

For five years my collection grew, filling several boxes, until 1979 when my head was finally turned by an attractive newcomer called *Match Weekly*.

I'm sorry I dropped you, *Shoot!*, and I'm even sorrier that we now live in a world where kids can't leg it down to the newsagents to eagerly pore over the latest issue.

FINLAND v. ENGLAND

Special features on this vital WORLD CUP QUALIFYING MATCH

SHOOT!

19th JUNE, 1976

12p

IN COLOUR
FOCUS ON JIMMY NEIGHBOUR TOTTENHAM

plus
ALAN HUDSON
BRIAN GREENHOFF
BRIAN ALDERSON
DREW BUSBY

ENGLAND

OR FAILURE?

...BER, 1969   1'-

ALAN HINTON
(Derby County)

BEHIND THE SCENES AT AJAX

SHOOT!
AND FOOTBALL STAR

22nd December, 1973

8p

MOBIL BADGES

We love these silk badges given away with Mobil petrol in the early '80s.

When was the last time you visited a petrol station to be gifted a football collectable that you thought was worth holding on to for 30 years, fer chrissakes?

Made of pure 100% silk from a silkworm's bottom * and, as such, suitable for stitching on to your Sunday best anorak or parka?

Free with four gallons of 4-star.

The only downside, associated more with the free giveaway poster than the patches themselves, was the prospect of a giant Alan Hudson marauding down the country like King Kong or Godzilla or worse – Dribble of Destruction Horror Shock – stomping down his non-shooting boot worryingly close to London.

Or some kind of cheap polyester.

'Snorting Ram', facing left: initially adorned DCFC shirts between 1971 and 1982.

RAM GAMBLE

You too can be a Rams Fiftyaire!

Never mind the flashy modern-day life-ruining tombolas giving away millions of pounds to undeserving twerps who just happen never to be us.

Now you can contribute 5 new pence (Subscription: 4½p; Voluntary Donation: ½p – sounds magnificently iffy to us!) to an unnamed cause related to Derby County Football Club, and see your hard-earned cash turned into premium biscuits to go with the directors' elevenses.

You too can go for a Golden Goal with the Rams, where the chances of the goal time coming up are strictly limited... but all for a good cause.

If you buy a goal-time ticket, you have a one second in 90 minutes chance of winning – that's 60 x 90 = 5400-to-1. Almost a certain winner. A surefire thing.

You too can check your ticket as soon as a goal flies in, to confirm that the time matches the one in your special sealed card. Practically a foregone conclusion.

Just one slight problem. The game ended Rams 0-0 Juventus.

Better luck next time, my old son.

BEARDIES

The natural state of man, and therefore footballers, is to be bearded; but the global daily assault by razors (with up to and including five blades) indicates that there are few cultures in the western world where a hairy lower face is the norm. From a high water mark in the mid-Seventies, beards have slowly disappeared from the face of British football.

We're not talking about a bit of lazy Wayne Rooney stubble here, but a proper beard. Months of growth, preferably with the same diameter as a piece of 13-amp fuse wire. A Roger Kenyon... a Trevor Hockey... a Frank Lampard... a Derek Hales... straight off the cover of *The Joy of Sex*.

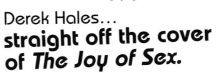

Derek Hales...
straight off the cover of *The Joy of Sex*.

Proper beards, for proper blokes.

Here's also to those players who binned the razor for a while but couldn't tolerate the fearful itchiness on a long-term basis: Steve Heighway, Martin Chivers, George Best, Colin Todd, Archie Gemmill ...at least they made a stand against the ultimately irresistible rise of Metrosexual Man, what with his hair gel and moisturiser and facial scrub.

118 DEREK HALES

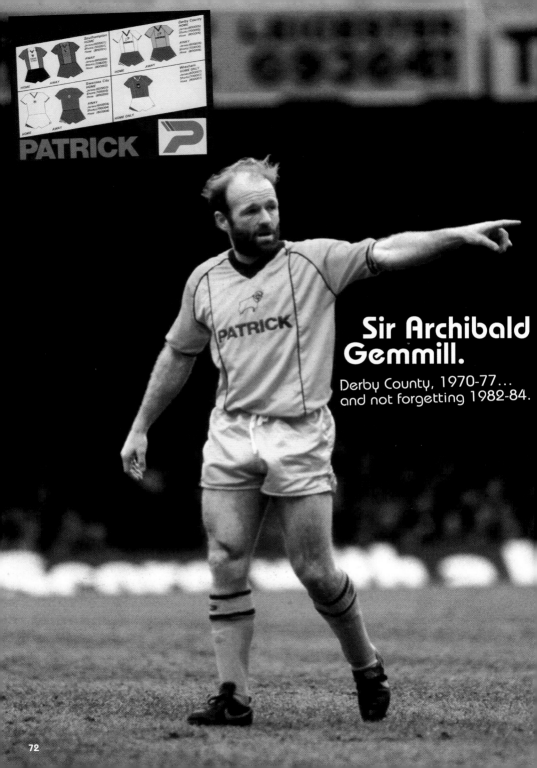

Sir Archibald Gemmill.

Derby County, 1970-77...
and not forgetting 1982-84.

PATRICK

French company Patrick Sportswear were known for their boots, trainers and kagoules before they began to produce football kits in 1980.

Southampton was the first one, which saw an interesting take on the Saints' stripes. Then, for the start of the 1981/82 season, Patrick made kits for Derby, Swansea and Wrexham.

The following season they added Birmingham City, Newport County and Rotherham United to their roster – all in their standard template.

Despite the limited range, the simple but pleasing design is fondly remembered by Rams fans, many claiming this was their favourite ever kit. The ram badge was flipped to be facing 'forward' and Patrick also stood in as shirt sponsor.

It was worn for three seasons, before Admiral came along to produce the Centenary strip.

C'est la vie...

RAMMY PIGGY BANKS

We've dug out an evocative article from a vintage 1968 issue of the *Football League Review*, which just happened to mark the first appearance on the market of the season-ticket saving aid which was to remain popular for years to come.

"Meet Rammy Banks," ran the introduction, "He is the latest and perhaps the neatest gimmick to be offered among an expanding range of goods being offered by League club shops."

"The demand is quite fantastic," said secretary Stuart Crooks of the Supporters Club brainwave manufactured by the Swadlincote pottery firm of Toothill & Co. "We are quite literally selling them while they are still hot from the kiln! Scores of our fans are using Rammy Banks to put aside money for next year's season tickets..."

Not bad for 10 shillings and sixpence.

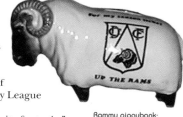

Rammy piggybank: Not a piggy, but a Ram. Clear enough?

PROPER COPPERS

When FKS finally produced their *Wonderful World of Soccer Stars* album and sticker set for a regional trial run in 1967, it's as if they were casting around for a method to stamp some Britishness on the very European feel of stickers, set against our good old cardboard oblongs. Deciding against introducing any actual stickiness to the self-styled sticker format – cue a million albums ruined by fumbly fingers trying to 'apply adhesive here' along the thin top strip on the reverse of the paper stickers – they apparently opted instead to include in the photo backgrounds as many good old-fashioned Bobbies as possible.

122 ROY McFARLAND

Dome-helmeted coppers staunchly patrolled the tunnel and touchlines, clearly watching the match instead of even pretending to keep an eye on the crowd. These were uniquely un-European football stickers, full of muddy kickaround action from old agency stock with cut-and-pasted heads – plus that vital ingredient of reassuring, trustworthy PC Plod.

It could never happen today, where all that's allowed into a card shot is a player's head and shoulders, with even club colours and badges blanked out unless all the correct merchandising licences have been fully paid up.

And even if the odd fluorescent-jacketed cop

117 CHARLIE GEORGE

did manage to sneak into shot, the effect just wouldn't be the same, with contemporary RoboBobs all weighed down by visors and pepper sprays, side-handled batons and laptop computers in the face of a silent, all-seated crowd of club clients.

There were no heat-sensitive cameras showing up in the background of even the most offensive perm and 'tache moments of the Seventies and Eighties; no helicopters taking to the air at the first sign of Graham Moseley's flappy back bit.

123 GRAHAM MOSELEY

"Oi, Moseley! I want a word with you!" Rams goalie exits sharpish over the white line.

The vital ingredient: PC Copper has a bit of a boogie.

FA CUP CENTENARY COINS

Good old Esso. Every year, they brought out something great for us to collect, and 1972 was no different. The handsome 'FA Cup Centenary 1872-1972' brochure and coin collection was such a must-have item for every young boy that silence must surely have descended on the forecourts of Shell garages while the offer was on, with tumbleweed blowing around between deserted BP, Jet and Cleveland pumps.

There were 30 of these "silver-bright, superbly-minted Centenary Coins" to collect, one per visit to the Esso station, the album to house them in representing a modest Dad Tax of 15p.

Swap yer 30 coins – from the Wanderers and Blackburn Olympic to the big gold-coloured centrepiece coin minted after all the others, a week after Leeds United's Wembley victory over Arsenal – all for the one Derby County coin commemorating that proud Saturday afternoon back in 1946. The Rams' greatest FA Cup moment in history... to date.

The Rams' greatest FA Cup moment in history **to date.**

OLD SKOOL TRAINING

We asked Rams legend Roger Davies about old-school training. There's famous documentary footage of Cloughie, which was reconstructed in *The Damned United*, at a training session where he's shouting: "You are a bloody disgrace..." Presumably Rog was at that session?

Kev lobs 'em over.
Franny bangs 'em in.
And not an A4 pad or
laptop in sight!

"Yes, I think it was Barry Butlin who took a corner because he was shouting at him and I scored a great volley from that corner from outside the box, and it was only a 5-a-side sized goal. But you don't see that, you just see him shouting: 'BAZ! You're a bloody disgrace'.

"We used to do all the hard running and fitness stuff with Jimmy Gordon and he used to hate it when he saw Brian coming over the hill because everything stopped and the ball would come out and we'd be straight into playing a game!"

Toddy: "Don't look now, lads...
**but I'm sure I just saw a giant
Rammy shaping up to jump
the crossbar."**

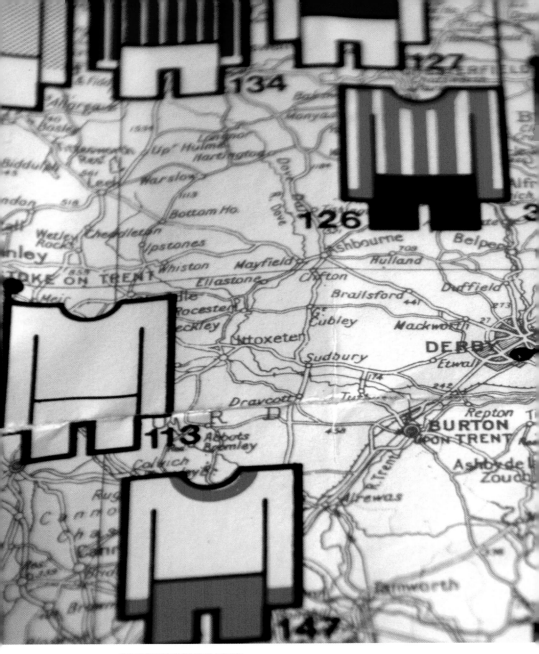

BARTHOLOMEW MAP

In the early 1970s John Bartholomew & Son produced the 'Football History Map of England and Wales' as part of their series of pictorial and historical maps… Created by John Carvosso, the stylised square kits and re-rendered club crests gave it an iconic look that remains hugely popular among football supporters. In the years just before more intricate kit designs arrived this was all that was required.

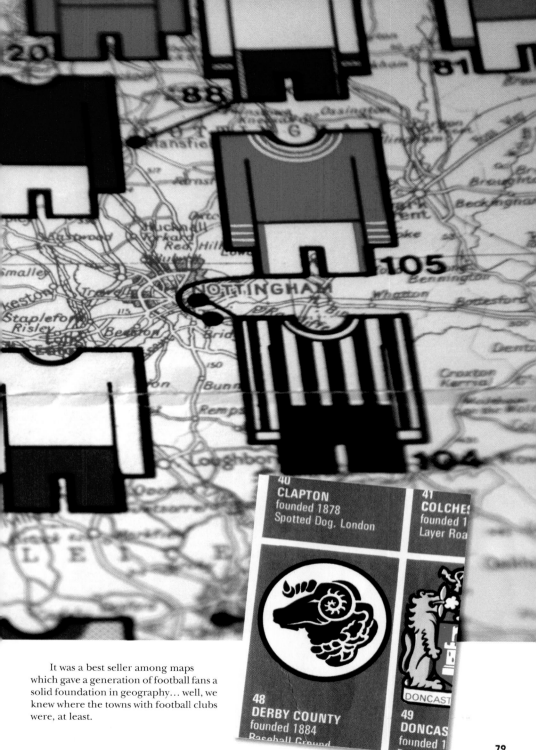

It was a best seller among maps which gave a generation of football fans a solid foundation in geography… well, we knew where the towns with football clubs were, at least.

SCOTTISH SUPERSTARS

Up until twenty years ago, every great First Division team in football history had included at least one Scot, usually the brains of the operation – the ball

Hearts, to slot conclusively into Clough and Taylor's jigsaw at Derby, and lead the Rams in turn to the championship. Taking over from Clough, Mackay then bossed the lads to the title in 1975, his team including Bruce Rioch and Archie Gemmill.

For the twelve years between the World Cups of 1970 and 1982, all of Britain took a special interest in the Scots as, time and time again, England failed to take the baby steps up on the

Oor Bruce and Oor Don, off to win the 1978 World Cup...

If there were a World Cup for value, Avenger would win it.

AVENGER

CHRYSLER
UNITED KINGDOM

The Chrysler Avenger. Style, toughness. And a Championship performance.

Wot, no Archie Gemmill?
No Joe Jordan?
No Graeme Souness?

player, the stopper who could do more than just stop, or the unstoppable goalscorer.

Whatever happened to the Scottish Superstar? There's no one now to stand alongside the likes of Dave Mackay, Kenny Dalglish or Billy Bremner.

Dave Mackay was the single most influential player in the Spurs side of the Sixties, and proved it in the supposed twilight of his career when he put off a cushy move, out to grass with

world stage. With so many familiar, gifted players, they became everyone's second team. Well, who were we supposed to support? Iran? The Scots heap derision on our temporary switching of allegiances thirty years ago. In the same position, they now wear 'Anyone But England' T-shirts, and we wouldn't want it any other way. But how sweet it would be to see Scotland return to dynasty-building form and make their first major championship this century; even back in the Home Internationals, so we can do our level best to beat their pasty bottoms.

Choose fitba.

Bruce Rioch

LEAGUE LINER

Specially commissioned by the well-meaning Football League, the League Liner express train was used to whisk lucky fans to away fixtures throughout the first half of the Seventies. Three hundred Burnley fans were the first to sample the delights of the on-board discotheque, the

Anthony Elliott of Coalville and Mick Cash of Shardlow celebrate with the Champagne that was distributed down the train

games room and TV lounge with footy on tape – and then the honour was shared around the supporters of every League club.

The buffet car was Champers class, and on-board variety entertainment was often laid on, featuring a comedian, singers and a high-kicking disco dance troupe.

The only down side: the main event of Stockport-Shrewsbury could seem somewhat tame in comparison.

"I remember going on the train from Derby to Arsenal in 1973," says Rams lifer Harry Seddon. "There might be football specials these days but they were certainly nothing like this. There was a disco on board, for one thing, with music piped through every carriage, and a very classy buffet car. There were singers and dancers on the inaugural trip."

Anticipating our doubting looks, Harry even sent some pictures of the train, in use by 300-plus Derby fans on a return trip to the capital. According to the captions, here's a couple of dancers from the Talk of the Midlands – blimey, never mind 'Show a leg, there'! – together with the nightspot's compere Ricky Disoni and sundry fans boogieing the night away on the way home to Derby.

Whatever happened to 'Anthony Elliott of Coalville and Mick Cash of Shardlow', who look like they can hardly believe their luck, having been handed a free bottle of Champagne by a high-kicking dolly bird!

Lordie be! That's what they used to call 'pre-match entertainment'...

Show a leg, there . .

FULLY PROGRAMMED

The Ram was the first tabloid-sized matchday programme and this newsprint groundbreaker persisted for around a decade, its lively red-top touches and unique appearance winning a place in fans' hearts, if not their back pockets.

The late Seventies and early Eighties saw something of a trend for newspaper programmes, with Rotherham United, Tranmere Rovers and Shrewsbury Town following Derby's lead.

It wasn't all good news for fans, who needed more elbow room on the terraces for their half-time read, and also for those of us who liked our prog collection of homes and aways neatly arranged in a box. This unnatural, unwieldy combination of two media had to be

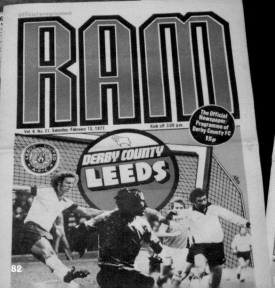

folded twice to fit in with the normal-sized ones. They got raggedy at the edges, turned sepia at the first hint of sunlight and then got brittle and started to fall apart. They were hardly in mint condition when you handed over your 20p, never mind when you got them home from the game. Enough to tip your average programme collector with OCD right over the edge.

Ultimately, the newspaper programme idea failed to catch fire

(unlike many of the programmes, which formed terrace bonfires and are now in short supply) and Derby abandoned the format in 1983, reconforming to the norm.

Needless to say, in this age of perfect bound and slickly produced all-the-same-size programmes, we now miss it and its unique character terribly.

MATCH WEEKLY

Saturday, May 17 1980 25p

Match Weekly was launched on 6 September 1979, three weeks into the 1979/80 season, by Peterborough-based publishers EMAP. Editor Melvyn Bagnall declared: "Our object is simple... to improve on anything currently available." By which, of course, he meant *Shoot!*, which had enjoyed a relatively unopposed decade of market dominance.

What immediately grabbed this 13-year-old about the newcomer on the newsagent's shelf was the way it was printed right to the edge, making *Shoot*'s white borders suddenly look very passé.

Inside there was a stellar line-up of writers: Keegan, Clough, Ardiles, Coppell, Atkinson and Jimmy Hill. Instead of 'Focus On' there was 'Match Makers', with loads more questions. There were more colour pages, and 'Match Facts' with marks out of ten for every player in every game. And, just in case anyone was still dithering about parting with their 25p, there was a free Transimage sticker album thrown into the mix.

After a five-year love affair with *Shoot!*, I jumped ship to *Match* in an instant. And I wasn't the only one. After a long battle, *Match* eventually won out with a higher circulation.

Match of the day before yesterday: Steve Carter leaps Forest hacker.

84

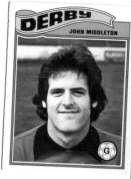

TOPPS

In 1938 a Brooklyn family business shifted their trade from tobacco to chewing gum... and never looked back. Topps were the company who gave us

Forest keeper John Middleton
transformed Superman-style
into Rams keeper John Middleton!

tiny 'Bazooka Joe' comics wrapped round their gum and, after 1975 when they took over A&BC, they provided us with our football card fix too.

The American takeover resulted in more garish colour-schemes for the cards and also coincided with the advent of more distinctive football strip branding. When Topps did get it right, and the 1978/79 collection with the team name on a banner is a favourite of ours, there is a classic pop-art quality to the cards.

Thanks to Andy McConachie of footballcardsuk.com for turning up this rare football card ephemera which provides evidence of Forest keeper John Middleton subtly being turned into Derby keeper John Middleton using what might have been the first ever version of Photoshop.

Trick or Tree? Now you see it, now you don't.

RAMTIQUE

There's a lot more going on down the ground than kicking a ball around these days. We're talking business-class banqueting, stadium tours, a members-only gym, conference facilities, unlimited retail opportunities and helicopter rides.

It's enough to make you yearn for the old-school souvenir shop, where they didn't sell corporate badged grooming sets (eyebrow notcher; beard sculptor; shower gel) or calendars of the playing staff printed last July, and already way out of date. No blue-and-yellow 'Thunderbirds' third kits, either, even if they do 'look good with jeans' according to the PR man. Hey, all sizes other than XXL and XXXL are reduced to a mere 30 quid! Which is to say, 50 quid to you.

Outside the Ramtique, 1975 – featuring Charlie George's haircut, 'after' and 'before'.

A 'flabbergasting' range
of terylene ties, Rammy piggybanks, ashtrays and ladies' fur hats
(Eskimo or pom types)…

Back in the day, the Ramtique club shop at 55 Osmaston Road was only the size of a two-berth caravan but gosh knows Mrs Jennings did a rip-roaring trade in Rammy piggy banks, plastic caps, sew-on patches and programme binders.

As club secretary Stuart Crooks said in 1969: there's a 'flabbergasting' range of goodies available. We're talking blazer badges (55 shillings), terylene ties (17/6), official club ashtrays (5/-) and ladies' fur hats (Eskimo or pom types) (19/11).

None of your new-fangled showy stuff like mugs, mind. And no need for bobble hats, because that's what grans were for.

Mackay says goodbye.
      Hmm, make that...
   "I'll be back."

MOTORING AWAY

The next time you set off in the motor car for an away match, why not leave the satnav behind and eschew the negligible pleasures of the motorway for the scenic route via a delightful daisy chain of A-roads? Yes, the experience may take you an hour or two longer, but think of the fun you'll have planning the night before with your trusty *AA Book of the Road*, earmarking roadside attractions and the finest transport caffs en route to Yeovil or Bournemouth & Boscombe!

One of the most enjoyable elements of the away trip is the camaraderie shared with fellow supporters, so be sure to make yourself instantly identifiable as a motorised football fan. Car coats and bobble-hat combos are tops in this respect, with a silk or knitted scarf in club colours recommended to be trapped flapping from your rear windows or quarterlights.

An amusing 'waving hand' novelty will win friends and influence the route taken by fellow away-trippers, so no wrong turnings. FOLLOW ME AND DERBY COUNTY, indeed! The match-day programme carries a set of directions to safely deliver us fans to next weekend's big fixture. Follow this expertly plotted route and there's

On the move with the Rams

ROAD RUNNERS' ROUTE to Manchester United next Saturday

From DERBY, take the A52 to Ashbourne, A515 via Newhaven to Buxton and continue along the A6 to Chapel-en-le-Frith . . . . 40 miles

A6 through Whaley Bridge, Hazelgrove and Stockport to Manchester, entering by Stockport Road (see Plan). Turn left along the B5093 and continue via Albert Road, Moseley Road and Wilbraham Road into Edge Lane. Turn right along the A56 Chester Road and then turn left along Warwick Road to Old Trafford . . . . 70 miles

Back to a time when motoring away **used to be a real expedition.**

every chance you'll end up sharing a glass-topped table with your heroes at a transport cafe en route.

Over a fried egg bap and a stewed cuppa, you will in all likelihood have the opportunity to discuss tactics with the starry likes of Ian Ormondroyd and Bobby Davidson, using the salt and pepper pots to represent oppo raiders.

And so, onward and ever upward, to the town or city of your destination, where the floodlights will safely guide you into the Victorian backstreets just a minute's walk from the away grandstand.

Happy motoring to one and all!

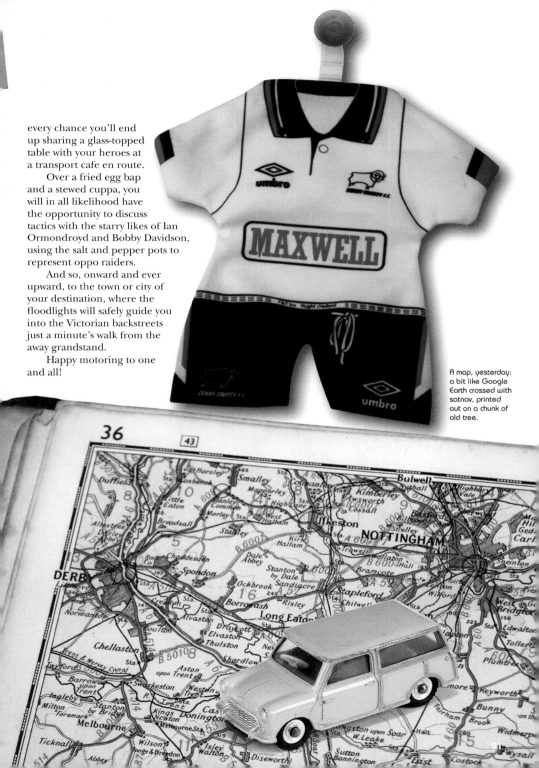

A map, yesterday: a bit like Google Earth crossed with satnav, printed out on a chunk of old tree.

RAMBEAT

Here's our unofficial Derby
County Top 10!

1 – 'Steve Bloomer's Watching'
*– Robert Lindsay and the
Pride Park Posse*
Has anybody got a cover or
sleeve pic of 'Wolfie Smith's'
proud anthem from 1979?

2 – 'Going Back to Derby'
– Rockin' Johnny Austin
The twangy Rams rockabilly classic
from 1968.

Never mind Liverpool, London and Manchester...
Derby is the home of all the greatest Rams-related grooves in history!

**3 – 'I Wish I Could Play Like Charlie
George'** *– The Strikers & Children
of Selston Bagthorpe Primary
School Choir*
There's no-one quite like
Grandma... or our Charlie!

4 – 'The Rams Song'
– The Carl Wynton Sound
The 1975 championship pub
singalong, oddly reminiscent of the
theme from *Only Fools and Horses.*

5 – 'We Will Follow You' *– Syndrome*
Brass band tiddly-om-pom-pom.

6 – 'Fan Fayre for the Commons People'
– Kev Moore
Released only a few years ago by the
Spanish-based Rams rocker!

7 – 'The Derby Rams'
– Mick Peat and Barry Coope
A whole seven-minute Rams history
in trad English folkie form.

8 – 'Forward Derby County'
*– Terry Ward with Trevor Antony's
Brass Foundation*
Primitive synthesizer sounds and a
reggae beat.

9 – 'Roy McFarland'
– Rockin' Johnny Austin
Elvis had nothing on the ever-
charitable Johnny, MBE!

10 – Urrryah *– ?*
Andy 'Relics of the Rams' Ellis recalls
a 1980s cassette release, with Derby
fans' chants worked into the track.
Got a copy?

Power to the
People! Robert
Lindsay as Wolfie
'Citizen' Smith,
with Rams scarf to
the fore.

SUN SOCCERSTAMPS

Long before the hilarious horrors of Sun Soccercards emerged at the end of the Seventies, *The Sun* newspaper bunged out a set of well-designed and sensitively considered collectables on an unexpected philatelic theme.

What we're trying to say is... they were stamps.

Sun Soccerstamps, to be precise. The equal best thing to happen in 1971, along with those Esso badges; but definitely more highbrow!

All this and eye-wrenching '3-D' freebies in the paper the next year, too!

One advantage of a white kit: Easy to colour in.

COLOUR ME BAD

Back in the day, I spent many hours scribbling away at the coarse paper of Caversham's Football Colouring Book, tongue lolling out to one side in sheer concentration, transforming the black outlines into lifelike and vibrant living colour. As you can see, I hardly ever went over the lines and had an almost eerie command of every stroke.

Derby's brilliant sunshine yellow, Everton's ultramarine, Liverpool's scarlet, Manchester City's forget-me-not blue (achieved by pressing not quite so hard on the ultramarine) were all portrayed to perfection under my artistic spell, now brought to life before your very eyes in a spectral rhapsody.

Just one tiny problem to prick my dreamlike bubble: "WHO'S GOT FELT PEN ON THE CARPET?!"

MAKE YOUR OWN BASEBALL GROUND

"It's the first time I've actually had it all together," says Andy Ellis of this magnificent cardboard model BBG we railroaded him into spending six solid nights putting together. "The stands were made, but I've never bothered to stick them on the base before!

"Did you know the model was available in two forms?" Andy adds, "complete as illustrated, or one where you could paint it yourself."

No, but we bet we know someone who's got both versions up in their shrine in the attic!

Blimey, it's enough to transport you directly back to the last days of the old ground, and the heart-wrenching move to Pride Park… which turned out to be not such a bad thing, after all. Even if the admission does run counter to everything we stand for nostalgically.

The model was available in two forms: with or without ankle-deep mud.

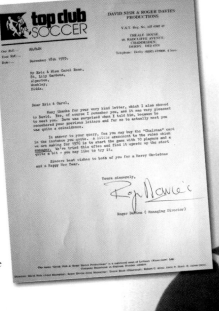

BORED GAMES

Thanks go out to Carol Jacques for sending us pics of her TopClub Soccer game, which has survived intact despite probably getting an airing every night – well, who could resist? – these past 39 years.

Carol describes it as "a board game of skill and chance for older children and adults of all ages, produced by David Nish and Roger Davies" – just two of the England internationals in the great Rams side back in the day.

Also included were two long, chatty and impeccably polite signed

A board game of skill and chance... produced by David Nish and Roger Davies

letters from Nishy and our Roger to Carol's late father, Eric Rose. The first, from August 1975, concerns a complaint about a missing game card, with David's excuses ranging from staff holidays, Roger's injury ("'op' apparently a success"), dispatching a

Top Club Soccer:
Derby County vs.
Derby County
in the Cup Final
every season!

car on a mercy dash to Heanor… and "strict training for Wembley".

Coincidentally, Wembley was also Eric and Carol's home address:

"Your kind comments concerning the game are much appreciated by both Roger and myself," David clattered away on his typewriter, "and I have already told several people about your daughter driving 260 miles to buy a game, which must, so far, be a record!"

In Roger's letter of December 1975, it turns out he's coincidentally bumped into Carol, who we can now declare the all-time record Top Club Soccer shopper!

Could it be time for an Xbox version of the game?!

Birmingham City
Founded 1875.
Div 2 1893, 1921, 48, 55.
FL Cup 1963.
Royal blue

Blackburn Rovers
Founded 1874.
Div 1 1912, 14.
Div 2 1939, FA Cup 1884,
85, 86, 90, 91, 1928.
Blue & white

Blackpool
Founded 1887.
Div 2 1930.
Div 1 runners-up 1956.
FA Cup 1953.
Tangerine & white

Bolton Wanderers
Founded 1874.
Div 2 1909.
FA Cup 1923, 26, 29, 58.
All white

Bradford City
Founded 1903.
Div 2 1908.
Div 3 (N) 1929.
FA Cup 1911.
Claret & amber

Brighton & Hove Albion
Founded 1900.
Div 3 (S) 1958.
Div 4 1965.
Blue & white

Bristol City
Founded 1894.
Div 2 1906.
Div 3 (S) 1923, 27, 55.
All red

Bristol Rovers
Founded 1883.
Div 3 (S) 1953.
Sky blue & white

Everton
ed 1878, Div 1 1891,
28, 32, 39, 63, 70.
Div 2 1931.
Cup 1906, 33, 66.
Blue & white

Falkirk
Founded 1876.
Sc Div 2 1936, 70.
Sc Cup 1913, 57.
Navy blue & white

Football Club Badges

The Esso collection of 76 famous football club badges.
When you've completed this card you'll have a permanent record of the most famous
football clubs in England, Northern Ireland, Scotland and Wales represented
by their unique and colourful insignias. Keep it safe - you will own what may become
a valuable collector's item.

EC European Cup. ECWC European Cup Winners' Cup. EFC European Fairs Cup. FL Football League. Sc Scottish. SLC Scottish League Cup.

Manchester City
ded 1894, Div 1 1937.
Div 2 1899, 1903, 10.
37, 66, FA Cup 1904,
56, 69, FL Cup 1970.
C 1970. Blue & white

Manchester United
Founded 1878, Div 1 1908,
11, 52, 56, 57, 65, 67.
Div 2 1936, FA Cup 1909,
48, 63, EC 1968.
Red & white

Sheffield United
Founded 1889.
Div 1 1898.
Div 2 1953.
up 1899, 1902, 15, 25.
Red, white & black

Sheffield Wednesday
Founded 1867, Div 1 1903.
04, 29, 30, Div 2 1900.
26, 52, 56, 59.
FA Cup 1896, 1907, 35.
Blue & white

Shrewsbury Town
Founded 1886.
Elected to League 1950.
Welsh Cup twice.
All blue

Southampton
Founded 1885.
Div 3 (S) 1922.
Div 3 1960.
Red, white & black

Stoke City
Founded 1863.
Div 2 1933, 63.
Div 3 (N) 1927.
Red & white

Sunderland
Founded 1879.
Div 1 1892, 93, 95,
1902, 13, 36.
FA Cup 1937.
Red & white

Swansea City
Founded 1911.
Welsh Cup 5 times.
Div 3 (S) 1925, 49.
White & black

Swindon T
Founded
FL Cup
Div 3 runners-
Red &

ESSO CLUB BADGES

What was your favourite set of freebies given away with petrol back in the day? Nowadays, it's hard to imagine anything but a form for a mortgage being handed out by the garage man, as it costs the same now to fill your tank as it did to buy your first car. But this hasn't always been the case.

While the likes of Texaco and Shell seemed obsessed with making huge amounts of money by flogging us the world's overflowing natural resources, back in 1971 good old Esso were only concerned with making sure that small boys had plenty of great football stuff to collect. First, there were World Cup coins, then 'Squelchers', a series of little booklets so named because the info contained in them was enough to squelch any argument. There were FA Cup Winners coins, and the Top Team Collection of Photo-Discs built a squad of Britain's best players... but best of all was surely the literally

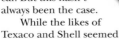

QUIZ BALL

Quiz Ball was a staple of early-evening BBC Light Entertainment from 1966/72, originally reffed by David Vine before Stuart Hall took over en route to *It's A Knockout* stardom. The general knowledge quiz set club against club, each fielding teams of three stars plus one celebrity supporter.

There were four ways to score a goal, ranging from four easy questions to one decidedly difficult one, the routes to goal being illuminated in 100-Watt bulbs on a big board. The oppo could try to steal the 'ball' by answering the other team's questions – at the peril of giving away a goal.

The lasting legacy of the series was the phrase 'Route One', the direct but tricky path to glory; but the smarty-pants players and guests also stuck in the collective consciousness. As, of course, did the Derby County team's splendid victory in the 1970/71 series, when they beat Crystal Palace 4-2 in the final.

Can any readers remember who was in the side, and who was roped in as the Rams' savvy celebrity superfan?

Rogues gallery: The *Quiz Ball* book's choice of cover stars was only unfortunate in retrospect…

titled 'Esso Collection of Football Club Badges'.

Esso even provided a splendid fold-out presentation card to stick them in and, frankly, if there was anything more exciting happening in 1971, we can't remember it now. It wasn't just the 20p blackmail job for the 'Starter Pack' of 26 otherwise unobtainable badges that made the heart beat faster. The little foil badges were irresistible. Everyone was collecting them.

Have you still got yours?

What price now, this vintage deluxe full-colour Champions! scaff?

SCARF ACE

The 1970s brought us so many new technological miracles, most of which had been unthinkable before the advent of the Space Race, the pressurised inventiveness of NASA and the resulting seven-iron shot on the moon. There was the digital watch with the numbers that glowed red; that tennis video game that went beep boop; video recorders and non-stick saucepans and portable calculators... and most astonishing of all, the unprecedented ability to print photographs onto fabric.

At first we had Six Million Dollar Man pyjamas and Osmonds T-shirts. Then Major Sports (Leicester) Ltd transferred the hot new technology to the football scarf market and 'picture scarves' were suddenly available for all the top club and Home International sides, up to and including Wales.

Who needed the Bionic Woman, the Bay City Rollers or the Wombles when you could have Dave Mackay, Leighton James and Charlie George's bubble-perm hung round your neck, portrayed in glorious polyester pixels?

BEHIND THE SCENES

If only it had been possible to open up the front of the main stand like a giant doll's house and peer in beyond the green bench seats, there would be the oak-panelled office where Brian Clough would shout huge numbers into his telephone, and make underperformers cry. The cigar-reeking lair of the director and his cronies. The echoey white-tiled changing room where players got their legs rubbed by middle-aged men. All unseen, invisible, off limits – for good reason, and forever.

Neither players nor officials nor employees of the club, we were mere mortals – and so would remain rightfully excluded. Our only route into this magical, off-limits world came via a set of club matchboxes featuring tiny pixel-heavy snapshots of the Promised Land...

All you need is an Adidas bag

(with 'all day I dream about sex' added in felt pen).

BAG TAG

During our time at secondary school we invented a game that was so good we were convinced it would be adopted by every twelve-year-old boy in the land, sweeping across Britain like a forest fire; but somehow it didn't.

All you needed to make dinner-hour a time of high-octane excitement was a tennis ball. The rest of the equipment you already lugged round with you all day. Your bag.

Whether the cheapo variety with 'Sports' printed on the side; or a pricier 'Adidas' bag (with 'all day I dream about sex' added in felt pen) we placed them in a circle, the size of which was determined by the number of players. The rules were simple, as indeed were we. You could only touch the ball with your feet. Your bag was your own individual goal. If the ball hit your bag you had one life

left – a second hit and you were out of the game. You had to strike a balance between defending your own bag and forming alliances to attack someone else's. There was plenty of scope for subterfuge and double bluff and just as in *Macbeth* (which we would be studying later that day in English), overreaching ambition could swiftly lead to your downfall.

The old school tie (complete with cool cig burn) – and the authentic DCFC trainer's kit bag.

ACTION TRANSFERS

This is easy. All you have to do is scribble the transfers off their greaseproof-paper backing on to the empty pitch in front of the Kop, and soon you'll have an action-packed Instant Picture™ of a match as good as anything a photographer could produce.

Now then. Let's 'peel away backing paper' and kick off with one of the Lilac team realistically booting the ball upfield. While his goalie jumps

The full glory of the transfer isn't captured
until they're artistically applied to a scene...

Complete this scene using some of your instant pictures.

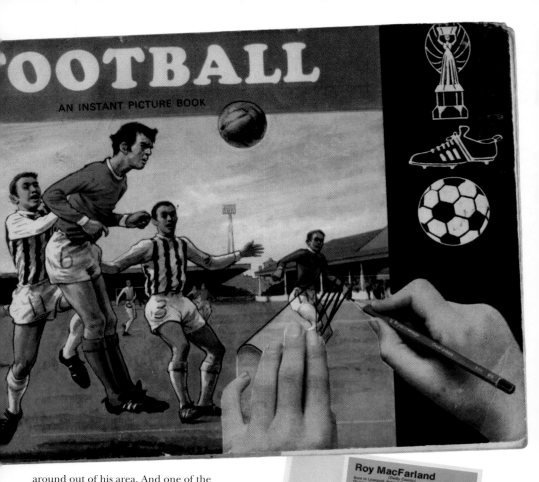

FOOTBALL

AN INSTANT PICTURE BOOK

around out of his area. And one of the Turquoises throws a dummy on the edge of the box. While another one goes for a diving header sitting on his team-mate's shoulders.

It's no use the Letraset bods flagging up the deadly danger of failing to 'slide backing paper under other pictures to avoid accidental transfer' – it's already too late for the centre-forward's head. What we really need is more players just hanging around, like in real life, gossing and blowing on their hands and doing leg stretches...

Roy MacFarland
(Derby County)
Born in Liverpool. Helped Tranmere Rovers win promotion to Division Three in 1967 and was transferred to Derby for £25,000 in 1967 (the record transfer fee ever received by Tranmere). Was in the Derby side which won promotion to the First Division in 1969. First capped for England against Malta in February 1971 and had won five caps in all up to the end of 1970-71 season.

Not me, guv! The ref was whistling for a foul on Lubanski before McFarland had even appeared on the pitch.

SPOT THE DIFFERENCE

1   There's a half-time Army brass band –
    last example spotted 30 years ago.
2   And there's a half-time scoreboard,
    with cunning A-Z code.
3   It's muddy. Very muddy. A 'mudbath'.
    Like it always was at the Baseball
    Ground.
4   Offiler's Ale sign up on the roof. You
    don't get adverts on stand roofs any
    more, let alone for Offiler's Ale…
5   You just get ads and corporate
    sponsor logos plastered all over the
    inside of the ground. But here there
    are none.
6   Policemen on the beat in amusing
    tit-style helmets, striding in comical
    slow motion around the cinder track –
    while small children whistle the *Laurel
    & Hardy* theme.
7   And no army of useless security-
    guard stewards clogging up the
    aisles, telling people to sit down.
8   An old-style, two-tier stand with the
    posh nobs in seats at the back and a
    proper standing 'paddock' in front.
9   That colour green used on the stands
    was only available pre-war.
10 Proper nets that you could stand
    behind and still see the match.
11 Tiny dugouts with fans surrounding
    them.
Sub And that'll be a ram by the touchline.
    Some things never change!

Now we want to get Europe again ....qui

EUROPE

We asked Andy Ellis, author of *Derby County: The Rams in Europe* to pick his all-time Top 7 Rams Euro spectacles. Of course, if you want the full stories, you know where to look!

1 - Airdrie (h): Texaco Cup final, 1971
Our first European trophy, and Roger Davies' first goal.
The first leg, in front of 16,000 at Airdrie in January 1972, was a goalless draw and Derby won the second leg 2-1 to lift the cup.

2 - Benfica (h/a): European Cup, 1972/73
The Rams' first real European test came against the giants from Portugal in the second round match, the Rams winning 3-0 at home then holding Eusebio and co to a 0-0 draw in Lisbon. Clough had the pitch dammed and filled with water after the last Benfica training session!

3 - Real Madrid (h): European Cup, 1975/76

The Rams won 4-1 at home but it was actually a very close game. For many fans it featured the finest ever DCFC goal – Charlie George's first. Charlie himself thinks that the goal he scored in Madrid was actually a better strike... even if the Rams did lose 1-5.

4 - Finn Harps (h): UEFA Cup, 1976/77
Dave Mackay's third foray into Europe as Derby manager proved to be the club's last in major competition. 12-0 against a very poor Irish side in the first round is still the club's greatest victory in any competition, but Dave's time was running out...

5 - Juventus (a): European Cup, 1972/73
The semi-final was a two-legged affair, the Rams going down 3-1 away then being held to 0-0 at the BBG. There are amazing stories of arguments between Clough/Taylor, Italians cheating and bribing the referee. Kevin Hector's goal was the first by a British team in Europe on Italian soil!

6 - Cremonese (Wembley final): Anglo-Italian Cup, 1992/93
Rams back in Europe and back at Wembley, but a busy season under Arthur Cox ended with a 1-3 loss under the Twin Towers. Cremonese were top of Serie A at the time.

Franny Lee wheels away in celebration after Charlie George's wonderstrike against Real Madrid.

¡Viva
el Derbyo Countyo!

7 - Atletico Madrid (a): UEFA Cup, 1974/75

The Rams' first ever penalty shootout in Mackay's first Euro campaign. The scores were 2-2 in both legs, but we won! The game finished at midnight – remember the classic Radio 2 commentary of the shootout?

DERBY COUNTY

The Rams in Europe

Andy Ellis

Foreword by Michael Dunford

Cheap holidays in other people's misery: Mainly Eusebio's.

RAM GURLZ

For men, aka large children, of a certain age, there was only ever one class of supporter to trump the legendary Sky Blue Girl of the Match draped over the back page of the Cov prog in 1972… gawd bless our Ram Girls of the Week!

We love you all!

Of course, there's a good chance that at least some of these lovely ladies are now the equally lovely mums or wives of someone you know, so best go easy on the just-pretend *Carry On*-style sexism!

Get in touch, and we'll be chuffed to send any of our Ram Girls of the Century a free book.

OH!, WHAT A GIRL

(But, oh!, what a shir

LOVELY model girl Tina tries one of the small baths in the Ram's dressing r Baseball Ground and looks beguiling. But that's because of the new-style R complete with the new diamond design, which is now available from the Ra Osmaston Road. They start at only £3.95. The whole strip, with shirts and s available from £6.95 in most popular sizes, including juniors. They're just a new

Here's ou
tractive
Derby Coc
TRACEY
JAYNE
JESSOP,
modelling
Derby Cou
bra, comp
with R
motif,
available
all sizes fr
the Ramti
at 55-8
Osmaston
Road. (£2.30

You'll fi
a comple
range
Rams goo
and souveni
at the Ra
tique an
from time
time th
season, we
feature
Tracey Jay

50,000

PARK

Girl of the week sends good luck wish for tonight

YES, IT'S OUR SUPER SUN PAGE 3 GIRL AGAIN

WE TOLD YOU about
Gillian Duxbury a couple
of weeks ago. She is the
page three Sun girl who
came second in that
newspaper's contest for

108

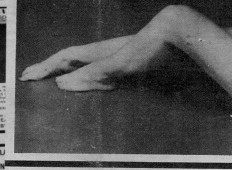

PRICE 60p

RAM MAGAZINE

Bass
MAIN
SPONSOR

OFFICIAL
DERBY
COUNTY
MATCHDAY MAGAZINE

epeata

s local

RAMS SENIOR SQUAD TEAM PICTURE IN FULL COLOUR: CENTRE PAGES

DERBY COUNTY v WOLVERHAMPTON W.
MONDAY AUGUST 26 1985

this unique transport system last season

NOTEL HAVE A SNACK

offer for the rby weekend

A RAMS BIKINI

FOUL

Running unevenly between 1972 and 1976, the effect of *Foul: Football's Alternative Paper* was to usher in the era of the fanzine.

For the first time, fans saw what was possible given a typewriter, a pot of glue and "a mountain of disgust" focussed hilariously on a game which the mag's editors perceived as mired in negativity, corruption and Don Revie.

Visually reminiscent of *Private Eye*, text-heavy with cartoons and stolen snippings from the overground press, *Foul* too dealt in parody and arsey farce, but its scope differed in that the majority of its targets – lazy hacks, cynical FA bigwigs, Don Revie – remained blissfully unaware of its existence.

Fans welcomed the new voice of football because it echoed their own passionate, romantic, gloriously pessimistic conversations in the pub and on the terraces.

"'Previous philosophers have interpreted the game: our task is to change it' – B. Clough (attrib)." – Foul, issue 1

Foul

THE ALTERNATIVE FOOTBALL PAPER 10p December 1973

Big "Chiv" – the rest of the row!

CHIVERS RIDDLE ROW FLARES ANGER FEAR SHOCK SHOT INQUIRY BIG DRAMA

But Chivers' goal against Manchester United the other week should have be safe for the fans should keep the understanding happy who are understandably puzzled by the shock decision.

WHO CARES?

Why Girls Prefer Goalies 250 TO BE W

WIN A NITE OUT WITH A SEX FIE

SEE PAGE 9

ATOM WAR MEANS ENGLAND COULD PLAY IN WORLD CUP FINALS!

See Back Page

FOUL

The Alternative Football Paper November 1973 Number 12 10p

CLOUGH SIGNS FOR US!

"I AM DELIGHTED TO JOIN FOUL MAGAZINE ON A FULL-TIME BASIS. THE EDITORS ARE BIG ENOUGH MEN TO EXPECT BY "ALTERNATIVE" FOOTBALL COVERAGE TO INCLUDE THE ALI-FRAZIER FIGHT IN NEW YORK, AND ENGLAND'S TOUR OF THE WEST INDIES, ON EXPENSES IF THEY DON'T LIKE THAT THEY KNOW WHAT THEY CAN DO".

Brian Clough

THE GREEN 'UN

This same ritual went on up and down the country for decades, little kids and old blokes queuing up outside the paper shop at 6 o'clock on Saturday night, waiting for the sports final edition of the local paper – the *Green 'Un*, the *Pink 'Un*, the *Blue 'Un* or the *Buff.* Any colour as long as it wasn't white. Here was sports journalism at its most demanding, where reports were phoned in on the hoof, assumptions were made before the final whistle, and last-minute goals were any editor's nightmare.

The *Telegraph Sports Final* match report
was vital reading
if you'd just left the BBG 80 minutes ago.

The *Derby Evening Telegraph Sports Final* was vital reading for those fans couldn't rest until they had read a report of a game that some of them had seen eighty minutes ago (unless they were after confirmation of a result they'd just heard played out on the radio).

The *Green 'Un* gave you the chance to settle down in a favourite armchair, to check the pools and peruse the results and league tables at your leisure. In the days before Sky News and even Ceefax, it was either this or wait for the arrival of the Sunday papers.

Gradually the need for a Saturday evening sports edition lessened and then disappeared altogether. The internet was one blow – suddenly you didn't need to be standing out on the street in January – but the killer was the spreading of fixtures over the weekend due to the demands of TV.

One by one, the sports papers had to admit defeat and hold up their hands in surrender, in Manchester and Liverpool, Derby, Leicester, Coventry, Birmingham... although the Norwich *Pink 'Un* and Ipswich's *Green 'Un* are both websites now.

If you can't beat 'em, join 'em.

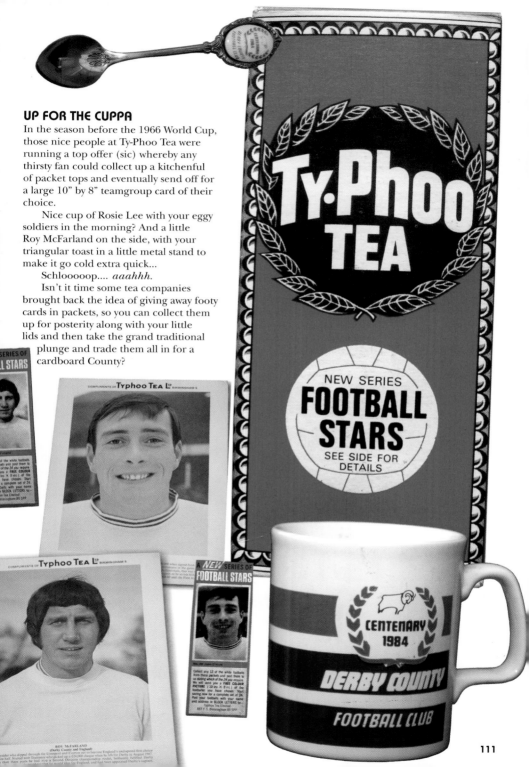

UP FOR THE CUPPA

In the season before the 1966 World Cup, those nice people at Ty-Phoo Tea were running a top offer (sic) whereby any thirsty fan could collect up a kitchenful of packet tops and eventually send off for a large 10" by 8" teamgroup card of their choice.

Nice cup of Rosie Lee with your eggy soldiers in the morning? And a little Roy McFarland on the side, with your triangular toast in a little metal stand to make it go cold extra quick...

Schlooooop.... *aaahhh*.

Isn't it time some tea companies brought back the idea of giving away footy cards in packets, so you can collect them up for posterity along with your little lids and then take the grand traditional plunge and trade them all in for a cardboard County?

Fire Safety Slogan

Bruce Rioch
5'11", 170 lbs. Sweeper

Alan Hinton says:
"Fire is a bad roommate; keep him off your team!"

David Nish says:
"CRAWL — That's the w to escape from a room fill with smoke; the air is bett near the floor."

SAFETY FIRST

Anyone who lived in Derby around the dawn of the 1980s will have noticed the sudden population drop when latterly white-booted winger Alan Hinton was installed as coach of the NASL's Seattle Sounders. 'Gladys' instantly signed up everyone in Derbyshire who could kick a football, provided they were over the age of 35!

We asked Roger Davies if it all seemed too good to be true, this extended working holiday in the sun... aka the NASL.

"There was a bit of that, but the football was of a decent standard, there were a lot of good players going to play out there. Off the pitch there was a lot going on and I suppose it was like a holiday then.

"You'd go away on a road trip for ten days at a time playing away games and it was really good fun. I had one year at Tulsa and then Alan moved to Seattle and took most of us with him. We had a fantastic three years at Seattle Sounders.

"I went back last year to pick up an award! I got a 'Golden Scarf' award thirty years after the event, for services to Seattle. They played Chelsea in front of 54,000 in their new ground."

So... did you play against Pele!?!

"Pele had just finished as I arrived, but I played against Franz Beckenbauer, Johan Cruyff, Carlos Alberto, George Best... it was the time when the NASL was at his peak. I then spent a year down at Fort Lauderdale with Keith Weller, we lived in the same complex. That was a good time too."

Alan Hinton
Team Manager/Head Coach

David Nish
5'10", 172 lbs. Fullback

Is that a multi-player mugshot concertina keyring in your pocket? Or are you just pleased to see me?

Jeff Bourne
5'9½", 170 lbs. Strike

Roger Davies
6'2½", 190 lbs. Striker

Bruce Rioch says:
"Once you get out of a burning building ... Stay Out :..Do not go back for anything!"

Roger Davies says:
"Don't play with matche and stay in the game — Lear not to burn!"

112

Arthur alert!
Don't fence me in.

"I'm not equipped to manage successfully without Peter Taylor. I am the shop window and he is the goods in the back."

Brian Clough

"We just gelled together, we filled in the gaps... My strength was buying and selecting the right player, then Brian's man management would shape the player." Peter Taylor

RAMS IN LIONS' CLOTHING

On arrival at Millwall for an away match, the Rams staff realised they'd forgotten their kit, and had to borrow Millwall's second strip. At least, so the story goes...

What's certain is that the Rams had just been crowned Second Division champions under Brian Clough, and ran out to a guard of honour made up of the Millwall team, all wearing Millwall shirts!

Which must have been a surreal sight for the baying crowd packed into the old Den.

Of course, it is possible that the Baseball Ground backroom boys simply forgot to pack the team's kit – though perhaps it's more likely that they merely forgot Millwall had changed to all-white, causing a clash, as the last several times Cloughie's boys had visited the Den, Millwall had been wearing blue shirts!

WILLIE CARLIN
DERBY

INSIDE LEFT

As luck would have it, the 1-in-a-million kit slip was captured for eternity on footy cards!

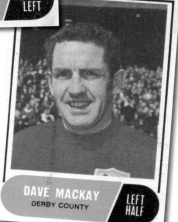

DAVE MACKAY
DERBY COUNTY

LEFT HALF

DAVE MACKAY'S TIES

When Cloughie made the inspired move of signing the veteran Dave Mackay from Spurs, he of course converted the triple FA Cup-winning skipper into a sweeper – delaying his move into management by just the crucial years it took to win promotion from Division 2, to be named joint FWA Footballer of the Year and help establish County in the top tier.

Mackay's enormous £14,000 signing on fee remains the stuff of legend – as

does Clough putting the great Scottish leader on £16,000 a year, more than Best or Greaves, Moore or Law. And there were other non-contract stipulations to be cleared up before Mackay would sign on the dotted line – such as a special dispensation to enjoy a sherbet on Monday through Thursday nights…and Cloughie moving training to Tuesdays so that Dave could have Sundays and Mondays off, to look after his Mackay's Ties business down in London!

STAND UP GEEZERS

When a young man was truly rather keen on football back in the day, it wasn't enough merely to cover all his bedroom walls with posters of his heroes, to drape the airing cupboard in scarves and badges, and to cover every available inch of shelfspace with football programmes, magazines and petrol freebies.

That still left the windowsill sadly bare and unadorned!

Which is where *Shoot!* came up trumps with these free-standing player figures given away with the mag in a spirit of generosity unparalleled today.

Dave Mackay

Derby County & Scotland

THE FOOTBALL CARD ENGINE

Here's how to transform your humble
pushbike into a revved-up, throbbing
beast of a motorcycle, all too easy to
mistake for a 750cc Norton Commando
(provided you're only listening rather
than looking).

Transform your pushbike into a Hells
Angel's Norton Commando

with Franny Lee's woody thrum.

All you need is:

1 – One giant pile of football cards;

2 – Two clothes pegs;

3 – An anti-social desire to terrorise
your neighbours like those cool Hells
Angels you've seen on *Nationwide*; and,

4 – A tragic disregard for your future
financial security.

If you've got a teetering pile of cards,
it naturally follows that you've got an
even bigger pile of swaps, collected up
over weeks of frustration while searching
for the two or three you need for the set.

We recommend you use a Franny
Lee 'red-back' from Topps's 1976/77
series. He's got a nice woody thrum.

All you have to do is use the
pegs to secure the cards on to
your bike frame so they stick
a little way into the spokes.
Then push off, taking note of
the unusual sensation of slight
resistance as you wobble down
the gutter, turning heads
with a guttural, engine-like
Vrrrrrrrrrp.

This way, in one afternoon
you might easily burn through
£100's worth of future sought-
after collectables at 21st-century prices.
But what the heck. You're only young
once, eh?

119

FIGHT!

We asked Rams legend Roger Davies about the Goal of the Month he won for his goal against Leeds – y'know, the game where all that anyone ever talks about is the big punch-up...

"Yes, I think I was on for the start of that game, although we had plenty of forwards then: there was myself, Franny Lee, Kevin Hector, Alan Hinton, all on the pitch, none of this one-up-front lark that people have now!

"I don't really have the same sort of rivalry, even hatred that they have for the Forest fixture round here. We hardly ever played them, not in my first spell here. I think Forest went down when we won the title in my first season here? So our big 'hate' game, because of the Clough v Revie rivalry, was always Derby-Leeds...

"They were really horrible battles. I was up against Norman Hunter who was a very hard man to play against. I got to know him and he is a really lovely guy, but back then it was a physical game and that's how Leeds played it.

You knew he was going to hurt you, but you had to give him one back to keep that respect up. Gordon McQueen was another one, he made his debut for Leeds against Derby and we were trying to get him, to welcome him to English football. It was a physical battle but I enjoyed it, I wouldn't have wanted it any other way.

"Football has lost something now, they've taken that out of it.

"I used to love sliding in on a right-back as he was about to clear the ball

and you'd take out man, ball, the lot. At best that would get you a yellow card now, so I'm not sure how long I'd last in the modern game!

"I think now there's a lack of definition between someone deliberately going for someone and a good, full-blooded challenge. You can't make every tackle. If someone does a bit of magic and whips the ball away in the last split-second then it should be a foul, but not a booking. I don't think it has improved the game at all."

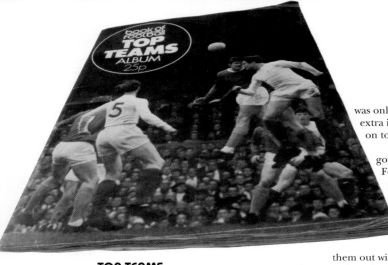

was only 6p at this time) an extra incentive was nailed on to the deal.

In part two you got this 'Book of Football - Top Teams' album and each week a sheet of 16 'stickers' in random order was issued. After carefully cutting them out with the big scissors from your Mam's sewing basket they were ready to be glued in.

They had you trapped now, for your quid a month.

Only when all your Derby heroes were present and correct on their page could you relax once more.

TOP TEAMS

In 1971, the good people at Marshall Cavendish, of Old Compton Street, launched their *Book of Football*, a part work encyclopaedia in 75 issues.

To ensure that you kept buying these weekly parts at a cool 23p (*Shoot!*

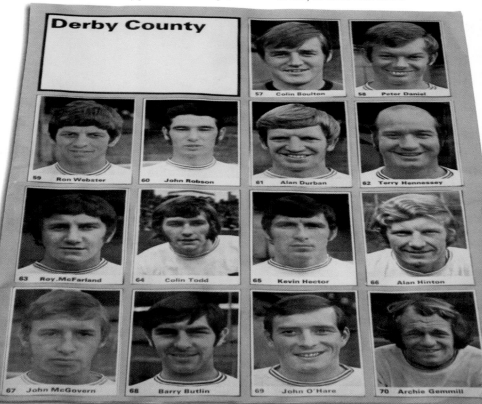

Derby County

57 Colin Boulton
58 Peter Daniel
59 Ron Webster
60 John Robson
61 Alan Durban
62 Terry Hennessey
63 Roy McFarland
64 Colin Todd
65 Kevin Hector
66 Alan Hinton
67 John McGovern
68 Barry Butlin
69 John O'Hare
70 Archie Gemmill

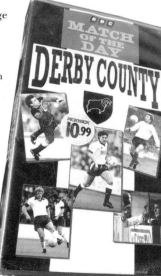

THE VIDEO AGE

Seldom has a new technology flared so brightly and died so quickly as video.

The race to develop a consumer-level video system was run in 1970s Japan, with JVC and their VHS eventually managing to overshadow Sony's Betamax system, and by 1978 the first video players were available in the UK. Available, but far from affordable for all but the spoilt kids.

Most families got one some time in the middle of the Eighties. It's pretty easy to work out because that's when our magpie collections of *Match of the Day* on Kodak E-180 tapes begins – not forgetting *Saint & Greavsie* and *Football Focus* editions snagged for posterity, when the ability to capture moving pictures off the telly box still seemed like something out of *Buck Rogers in the 25th Century*.

Whether painstakingly taping goals from the regional news, or building up a video library that could be measured in yards, it was an obsessive, and ultimately a pitifully pointless exercise.

No one now plays their rare early white-label editions of black-and-white match footage from County's successes in the late Sixties, never mind *Danny Baker's Own Goals and Gaffs* and the endless run of season highlights from seasons that somehow now seem to all run together in the mind. They're all out in the garage now, along with the precious unplayed vinyl and the music cassettes and the slideshow projector and the magic vegetable peeler gimmicks, still mint and boxed up the same as the day you bought them.

One day, the plan is to get a special machine where you link it up to your computer and convert them all into DVDs. One day...

A rare and collectable videocassette, yesterday: 50p for ten at every car boot sale.

GOAL LINES

Something on your mind? Drop a line to GOAL Lines. Praising or panning, it doesn't matter. £2 for Star Letter. Address: GOAL Lines, GOAL, 161/166 Fleet St., London. E.C.4.

Dear Editor . . . A STAR LETTER

GOAL

Modestly subtitled 'The World's Greatest Soccer Weekly', *Goal* launched on 16 August 1968, with a right posh do at the Savoy with dolly birds and everything.

Its distinctive covers, with a bright yellow title on a red background and circular photo design, owed a nod to pop art, and they've stood the test of time, still looking fresh and bold to this day.

'Opinion' kicked things off – "There is no sitting on the fence with Tommy Docherty. You are either for him or very much against him" – though 'Bobby Charlton's Diary' was the undoubted star turn.

Amid more distinctively designed colour posters and serious football features, 'Booter', the Beatle-haired footballer starred in his own cartoon strip, and we got to 'Meet the Girl Behind the Man'.

Goal became a victim of its own success because exactly a year later, encouraged by decent sales, IPC introduced a second football weekly, entitled *Shoot!*

Although both went on to achieve healthy circulations of around 220,000 by 1971, *Goal* then went into decline, and its 296th and final issue came out two weeks before the start of the 1974 World Cup.

It was then 'incorporated' into *Shoot!* which was akin to having to sleep under your little brother's bed.

Oh, the indignity.

Dave Mackay holds up Derby's championship trophy and signals his own return to Soccer's top flight

Now we are with best in the world says Derby's BRIAN CLOUGH

DESPITE THE trouble and torment experienced by most sides promoted to the First Division in recent years, Derby manager Brian Clough is confident his players can at least hold their own in a division he rates "the best in the world".

Nobody would disagree with that assessment and most people would agree that Derby probably are better equipped for the top of the pile than many of the clubs who have found themselves in exalted company recently.

Clough, two years in charge at the Baseball Ground — where he moved after a spell managing Hartlepool — is a thoughtful, forward thinking man who combines a confident outlook with a realistic appreciation of the facts of football life.

in the business. "In a way," says the manager, "Mackay without McFarland would be like eggs without bacon."

Certainly the experience of Mackay has had much to do with the great progress of McFarland in the last twelve months. And his inspiration as skipper has made a tremendous impact on a young Derby team.

Clough subscribes to the view most of his colleagues share that the First Division is becoming more and more like two divisions — the elite and the rest.

"There are six or eight places towards the bottom where we can hold our own quite comfortably at

First Division jitters? Not for Dave Mackay

124 DAVE MACKAY took one look at Derby's record—more than 70 goals against—and their position —fifth from the bottom of Division Two—and decided that this team

gap successfully. I really believe that."

Captain of Hearts at 21, captain of Scotland at 23, later captain of

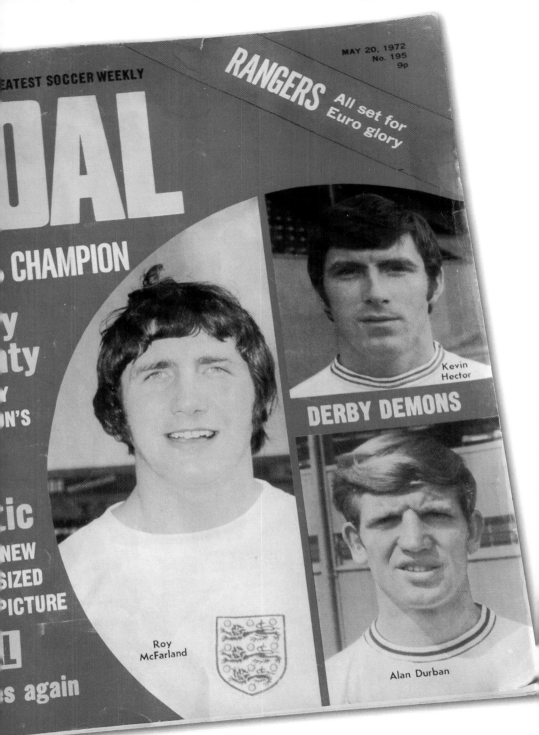

GREATEST SOCCER WEEKLY

MAY 20, 1972
No. 195
9p

RANGERS All set for Euro glory

GOAL

CHAMPION

y
nty
y
N'S

tic

NEW
SIZED
PICTURE

L

es again

Roy McFarland

Kevin Hector

DERBY DEMONS

Alan Durban

CHANGING TO YELLOW

Nowadays, it appears that every football marketing man's erotic dream is an all-black second strip, perhaps with a sparing, luminous-green or pink trim. But there was a time when it was absolutely *costume de rigueur* to wear a yellow away kit – or 'amber' as the Umbro

Leeds were probably the first – no, come to think of it, we realise it was almost certainly Derby – but by the late Seventies it seemed that every club that had to change kits were trooping out of the tunnel like a bunch of bananas. These were more practical times and this

wasn't done to sell shirts, but to avoid
the need for a third kit as so few teams
had yellow as a home strip.

Arsenal, Sunderland, Chelsea,

mustard/sunflower/canary/lemon/saffron
by the early Eighties, before someone
worked out that there might be money
to be made from more frequent colour

MAY THE CIRCLE BE UNBROKEN

The recent history of football has seen some pretty audacious cash-raking schemes instituted by football clubs under the free-for-all auspices of the Premier League. But back in a far more innocent age, an early marketing guru at Derby County proved to be way ahead of the game with the cash-raising idea of the 20th century:

"Let's take small amounts of something we've got tons of, that we're desperate to get rid of... and sell it for hard cash!"

Back in 1975, the BBG was being dug up and relaid for the umpteenth time in an attempt to transform the old quagmire into a luminous green front lawn. Eureka! The word of the day was 'encapsulation'!

The big idea was to sell 10,000 lumps of mud in a fancy plastic container with an antique-style certificate of authenticity – proudly signed by chairman Sam Longson and go-getting secretary Stuart Webb, presumably the 'brains' behind the scheme.

History doesn't record how many wheelbarrows of mud were sold; but the vast majority suffer from the plastic packing having broken down over the intervening years.

It was marketing genius, in unmistakable 1970s style:
Let's sell the BBG mud!

A&BC TEAM POSTERS

We've already mentioned some of the rarities that came free with the football cards and the fossilised stick of pink bubby gum in A&BC packets back in the day.

The little team posters of 1970 vintage were one of the most popular 'little extras' at the time, and because they were so flimsy and so regularly Blu-Tacked straight on to the shrine wall, they're almost impossible to find in mint condition, and can go for silly money on eBay.

As a follow-up to the freebie extra posters (which were folded up, four times the size of a regular card), in 1973/74 A&BC tried a standalone set of bigger posters (folded up six times) – and they proved one of the least popular items ever released by the company.

However, for precisely that reason, if you happen to have a drawerful of old ones in mint condition, the sherbets are on you!

The Rams, 1970:
Every one's a winner.

COLIN BOULTON
RON WEBSTER
JOHN ROBSON
ROY McFARLAND
TERRY HENNESSEY
COLIN TODD

THE DERBY COUNTY

ARCHIE GEMMILL
KEVIN HECTOR
JOHN McGOVERN

LEARN THE GAME

Drop whatever you're doing! The morning paper! A big creamy-topped pinta of milk! It's time to learn the art of cover defence courtesy of Colin Todd and those nice people flogging haystacks to small children as 'Shredded Wheat'.

It's simple.

Here Rod Thomas is covering the opponent with the ball and showing him down the line. My position is near enough to Rod to stop him taking him on man for man but far enough away to prevent him playing past us both.

Note the angle as well. See how it's changed now?

Look, put down your cuppa and concentrate, will you?

Next Week:
Colin Todd's breakfast seminar on the science of hacking down nippy wingers.

FLOODLIGHTS

Head tilted up to the heavens, the sight of a squally shower swirling through a floodlight beam was as close to God as many a football fan would ever get. Especially if the floodlight pylon (and the Supporters' Club bar) that had given rise to his epiphany were an afterthought addition to a crumbling barn of a terrace.

The floodlight pylon was an object of awe, towering hundreds of feet over the crowd, hemming in the oblong mudbath with its three brothers – naked iron-girder scaffolds tapering up into low cloud.

You have to look up to experience an intimation of the infinite, and your own insignificance. Hence church spires. City skyscrapers. Suicide pacts from suspension bridges.

And they were useful, too. How else was it possible to home in on an oppo ground on a 1970s Saturday motoring excursion? Seek the floodlights, and ye shall find.

PLAQUE ATTACK

Collect the big names now! And, with all due respect to Darlington and Southport, some of the smaller ones, too.

Once you'd cut out your first token from this *Shoot!* advert, ripped another off a fish-finger box and painstakingly assembled 25 new pee, then you were ready to send off and claim your embossed football club plaque from the Co-op.

Luckily Derby made it on to this seemingly random list of 31 large, medium and frankly tiddler-sized clubs... It's All at Your Co-op... NOW!

However, somewhat oddly, these vital tribal territory markers were also presented as a Ty-Phoo Tea promotion a year later, in the 1972/73 season, with a similar wedge of two tokens and 25p required.

Stick this to your bedroom door with four foam Sellotape sticky fixers and that baby is never coming off in one piece...

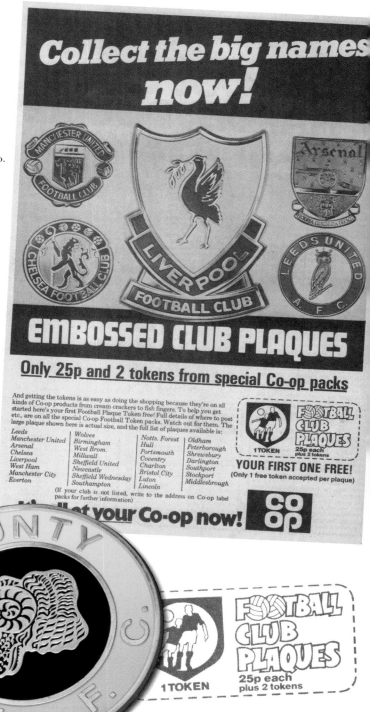

Collect the big names now!

EMBOSSED CLUB PLAQUES

Only 25p and 2 tokens from special Co-op packs

And getting the tokens is as easy as doing the shopping because they're on all kinds of Co-op products from cream crackers to fish fingers. To help you get started here's your first Football Plaque Token free! Full details of where to post etc., are on all the special Co-op Football Token packs. Watch out for them. The large plaque shown here is actual size, and the full list of plaques available is:

Leeds	Wolves	Notts. Forest	Oldham
Manchester United	Birmingham	Hull	Peterborough
Arsenal	West Brom.	Portsmouth	Shrewsbury
Chelsea	Millwall	Coventry	Darlington
Liverpool	Sheffield United	Charlton	Southport
West Ham	Newcastle	Bristol City	Stockport
Manchester City	Sheffield Wednesday	Luton	Middlesbrough
Everton	Southampton	Lincoln	

(If your club is not listed, write to the address on Co-op packs for further information)

It's all at your Co-op now! CO-OP

FOOTBALL CLUB PLAQUES
1 TOKEN 25p each plus 2 tokens
YOUR FIRST ONE FREE!
(Only 1 free token accepted per plaque)

FOOTBALL CLUB PLAQUES
25p each plus 2 tokens
1 TOKEN

DOING PENNANTS

Curiously, it's only two classes of games at either end of the importance spectrum – big European matches and Cup Finals, and utterly meaningless friendlies – that attract the attention of the club pennant maker, who provides the skipper with a long triangle of plasticky silk hanging off a length of dowling to hand over to the oppo captain before the toss-up.

Ever was it thus, though exactly why it's impossible to say. It was something to hang in the trophy cupboard during those long barren spells, we suppose. Treasured mementoes of clammy handshakes before the hacking began.

Far more fun than the official jobbies are these cheap plastic pennants designed for children to hang on their walls with less just-pretend po-faced ceremony. It's the ones that you could buy off the market for tuppence which are now worth most to collectors. The ones with the worst-drawn images of silverware and stars, and only partially accurate lists of trophies won before you were born.

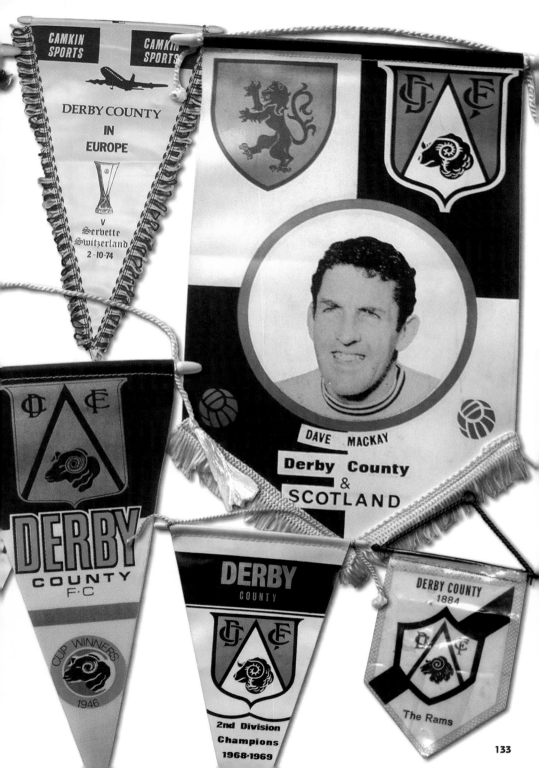

CAMKIN SPORTS

CAMKIN SPORTS

DERBY COUNTY IN EUROPE

V
Servette
Switzerland
2-10-74

DAVE MACKAY
Derby County
&
SCOTLAND

DERBY
COUNTY
F·C

CUP WINNERS
1946

DERBY
COUNTY

2nd Division
Champions
1968-1969

DERBY COUNTY
1884

The Rams

UMBRO

Umbro had been making fantastic football kits since 1924, when the HUMphreys BROthers Harold and Wallace set up a workshop in Wilmslow, Cheshire. In those less ostentatious days labels were worn on the inside of clothes, not the outside, so their prestigious list of classic kits remained largely anonymous.

Blackpool's famous FA Cup triumph of 1953, Tottenham's 1961 Double, England's World Cup glory in 1966, Celtic's European Cup win in Lisbon in '67 and Manchester United's the following year were all achieved in Umbro kit, with not a visible diamond in sight.

Umbro were the first to produce a full set of football kit replicas for kids in 1959, which became hugely popular when Denis Law endorsed them in the mid-Sixties.

By the time I was taken into our local sports outfitters for my first football kit, circa 1973, they were called the 'Umbroset' and came in a box with a cellophane front, affording you a tantalising glimpse of the shirt, shorts and 'hose' contained within (as they weren't interchangeable, you had to be 'average' size and keep your fingers crossed).

The first little logo
appeared on Derby County shirts in 1973.

134

By the mid-70s, branding was beginning to creep in and the first little diamond logo appeared on Derby shirts in 1973. By the eve of the 1976/77 season things had mushroomed and an advert appeared in *Shoot!* proclaiming: "It's going to be a sparkling season... just look at those diamonds!"

Six years after Brazil had won the 1970 World Cup in Umbro without a single diamond showing, the new range of Umbro kits now sported dozens, with multi-logoed tape down the sleeves and shorts, and Derby were in the vanguard.

However, Umbro were dropped in favour of Le Coq Sportif in 1978 and it was nine years before Derby sported the diamonds again. This time the side who had just returned to the top flight in 1987/88 wore a very tasteful round button up collar and shadow weave chequerboard shorts.

Umbro came up with two more decent designs for Derby, returning to the traditional colours of black and white (and a less popular third colur of red), before being replaced by Bukta in 1993.

Sadly, having been swallowed up and spat out by American giants Nike, Umbro's future looks to be in some doubt. It's probably just as well that Harold Humphreys – described as "the Dior of the football world" by the *Daily Express* in 1963 – isn't still around to witness what might be the double diamond's demise.

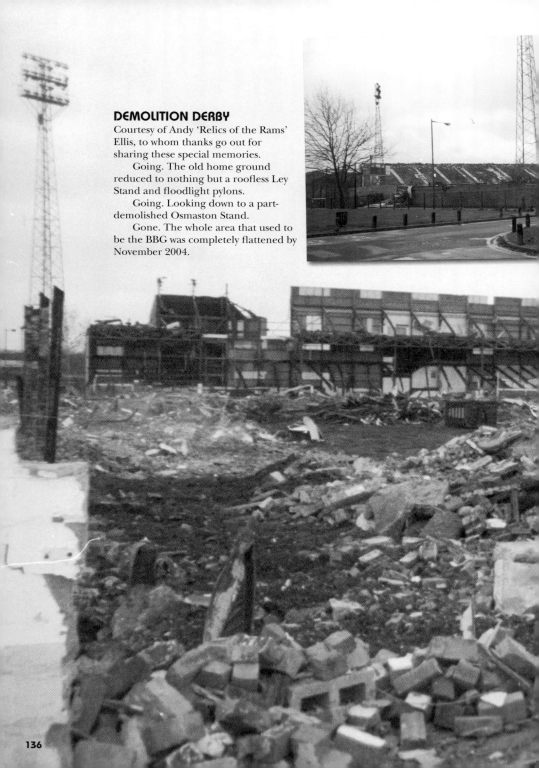

DEMOLITION DERBY

Courtesy of Andy 'Relics of the Rams' Ellis, to whom thanks go out for sharing these special memories.

Going. The old home ground reduced to nothing but a roofless Ley Stand and floodlight pylons.

Going. Looking down to a part-demolished Osmaston Stand.

Gone. The whole area that used to be the BBG was completely flattened by November 2004.

MOVING HOME

The 1997 time machine on the previous spread is enough to whisk you back to the Nineties.

"The Rams came a long way during the decade," says Andy Ellis. "From Division One under Robert Maxwell up to eighth in the Premier League by the end of 1998/99. There was Wembley, the last of the BBG and promotion to the Prem. It was a rollercoaster ride with a fantastic cast list including Arthur Cox and Roy McFarland, Jim Smith and Steve McClaren; Stimac, van der Laan and Willems. The ground move provided a superb setting for Premier League football, and Jim Smith

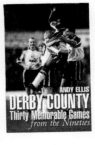

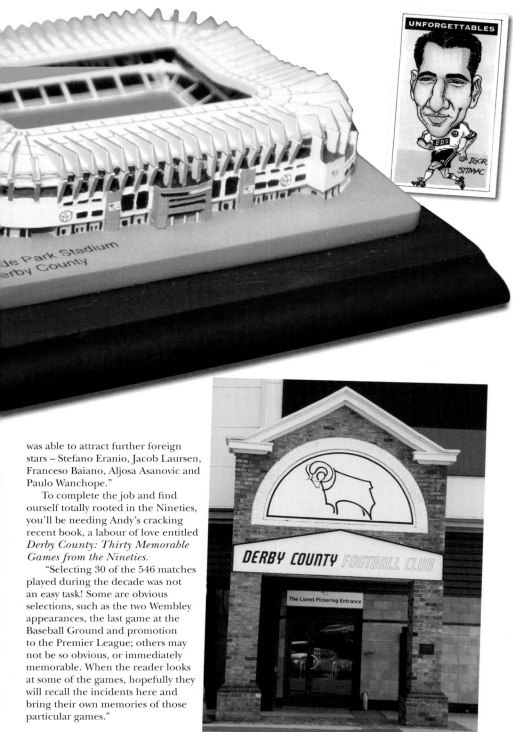

UNFORGETTABLES

IGOR STIMAC

de Park Stadium
erby County

DERBY COUNTY FOOTBALL CLUB

The Lionel Pickering Entrance

was able to attract further foreign stars – Stefano Eranio, Jacob Laursen, Franceso Baiano, Aljosa Asanovic and Paulo Wanchope."

To complete the job and find ourself totally rooted in the Nineties, you'll be needing Andy's cracking recent book, a labour of love entitled *Derby County: Thirty Memorable Games from the Nineties.*

"Selecting 30 of the 546 matches played during the decade was not an easy task! Some are obvious selections, such as the two Wembley appearances, the last game at the Baseball Ground and promotion to the Premier League; others may not be so obvious, or immediately memorable. When the reader looks at some of the games, hopefully they will recall the incidents here and bring their own memories of those particular games."

From us to you: Have a very happy Christmas, and a splendid New Year in 1987.

XMAS MORNING

Our 1970s Christmases, in our terrace front rooms and boxy housing-estate semis, weren't quite the same as the sumptuous Victorian festivals portrayed on Christmas cards and chocolate boxes, in TV ads and cartoons.

We didn't have stockings hanging from huge holly-bedecked fireplaces. We had striped pillowcases stuck on the end of our beds.

We didn't have gaily laughing guests – gentlemen in top hats and ladies wearing furry muffs – we had bald men round in their new V-neck jumpers, and they hardly spoke.

And we had, to be frank, shite artificial Christmas trees, not those towering, richly decorated spruces portrayed on the cover of the *Radio Times*.

As for the romantic notion of a White Christmas, it never snowed round our way; though sometimes it rained.

Christmas dinner was the same as normal Sunday dinner, except with turkey instead of roast beef, and with added parsnips and sprouts. Rather than the mouthwatering spreads portrayed ... well, you get the idea.

But somehow, on Christmas morning, with Noel Edmonds visiting children in hospital as a televisual backdrop, we still managed to reach a goosebump-inducing level of excitement.

And it was all because we knew that, concealed in cheap Woolies wrapping paper, piled up under the shite tree, there lurked *Shoot!* annuals, Wembley Trophy footballs, full football strips and Subbuteo accessories housed in their pale green boxes.

So we never took a horse-drawn sled down to the pine forest to chop down the tallest tree to place by the main staircase like those privileged Victorians... but then, they never had Subbuteo Team No. 10, did they?

We never had sleds and holly-bedecked fireplaces
but, then, they never had Subbuteo Team No. 10, did they?

Authors

Gary Silke and Derek Hammond are the authors of *The Lost World of Football* (Pitch, 2013); *What A Shot! Your Snaps of the Lost World of Football* (Pitch, 2013), and *Got, Not Got: The A-Z of Lost Football Culture, Treasures & Pleasures* (Pitch, 2011).

Picture Credits

Andy Ellis and Andy McConachie at The Derby County Collection:
Cover, 5, 6, 10, 14, 18, 19, 21, 26, 28, 29, 31, 34, 36, 37, 40, 41, 42, 48, 50, 51, 53, 56, 58, 58, 59, 62, 63, 64, 66, 67, 71, 73, 76, 77, 80, 82, 83, 85, 86, 87, 88, 90, 91, 92, 93, 95, 100, 101, 104, 106, 107, 111, 112, 117, 118, 123, 126, 128, 130, 131, 132, 133, 136, 137, 139, 140, 141, 142, 143, 144.
Neville Chadwick Photography: 54, 72.
Getty Images: 20, 113, 120.
Vectis Auctions – collectible toy specialists, www.vectis.co.uk:
58 (ice-cream van),
91 (Austin Countryman).
Carol Jacques: 96, 97.
Kare Bjorklund: 129.
Steve Marsh: 111 (box)

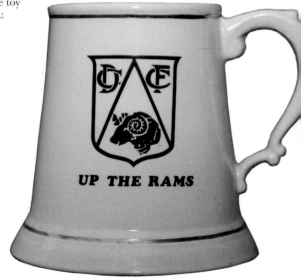

Acknowledgments

Grateful thanks to Andy Ellis and Andy McConachie at The Derby County Collection for all their help assembling the memories and memorabilia in this book.

David Tossell for the Swivel Boots ad.

Paul Woozley for the Mobil poster.

Thanks also to Nigel Mercer for his Lion league ladders and Letraset. Check out his ace, encyclopaedic football card and sticker website at cards.littleoak.com.au.

And, if you're a Letraset fan, the SPLAT Archives at action-transfers.com.

About The Derby County Collection

A quick look around the iPro Stadium shows remarkably little for 130 years of football. A conservative estimate of 90% of all Derby County-related material is in private collections where it is likely stored in lofts, garages and storage units and is seldom seen or displayed.

The Derby County Collection is a state-registered charitable trust, independent of the club, with some initial aims and targets – to act as the authority on all matters regarding the history, its ephemera and collections; to assist and advise DCFC in presentation of material and matters concerning the club's history; to encourage the preservation of the heritage of DCFC; to research, document, digitise and catalogue to international museum standards; to arrange displays and exhibitions; to maintain safe custody of materials entrusted to it; to stimulate interest and provide educational material for schools and community groups; and to attract external funding.

The long-term goal is to have a permanent home for The Collection – preserving the heritage of The Rams for the fans, for the club and the City.

To find out more and to get involved: www.derbycountycollection.org.uk
or email: administrator@derbycountycollection.org.uk
Twitter: @dcfccollection

More Critical Acclaim for *Got, Not Got*

"This exquisite book is a homage to the game of 40 years ago – not just the mudheaps and the mavericks but a celebration of its wider culture [which] rises above lazy, modern-life-is-rubbish nostalgia...
The design is so sumptuous and the stories so well chosen and written that it's hard to resist the authors' conclusion that much – call it charm, character or even romance – has been lost in the rush for cash. Regardless of whether it really was a golden age, this is a golden volume, as much a social history as a sports book. If you've not got *Got, Not Got*, you've got to get it."
Backpass

"I can guarantee that virtually anybody who flicks open this magnificent book will immediately want to have it."
The Football Trader

"For further reminders of the long-lost game of the 1960s, '70s and '80s, the illuminating new book *Got, Not Got* does a very fine job."
Sport magazine

"If, like myself, you are an unashamed nostalgia junkie, this book is for you.
It's more than just a book on football collectables, including memories and experiences from the golden age – a time before the FA Premiership and TV money took us through a pound-sign portal and into a parallel, but much less likeable, universe. Some of my favourite experiences/memories are included – I found myself saying either 'did it' or 'remember it' – and there's a heck of a lot to choose from."
Programme Monthly

"A huge success and an epic tome for lovers of football nostalgia everywhere."
The Football Attic blog

"It's an absolute beauty."
Adrian Goldberg, BBC Radio WM.

"An absolute gem of a book – part brilliantly written lament for an earlier age, part opportunity to reminisce about a time when you hankered after a Garden Goal ('Every Boy's Dream!')...
Football's relentless commercialisation comes, naturally enough, at a cost. It's brought us everything from the Stalinist-style obliteration of the game's pre-1992 history to the modern player, kissing the badge, logo and sponsor's name after scoring. A purer, less cynical era is depicted throughout *Got, Not Got*. Buy it – you will not be disappointed."
SportsBookoftheMonth.com

"The best dose of retro football nostalgia ever. I can't put it down!"
footballcardsuk.com

"It's a beautiful book – a smorgasbord!"
John Keith, City Talk FM, Liverpool

"An exhaustively researched collection of football programmes, stickers, badges and memorabilia, a coffee table book you can dip in and out of at any time. Some of the advertisements from old programmes are classics – 'Bovril – hot favourite for the cup!' Or culinary advice to players: 'Full English – eat up your fried bread now, it's full of energy.' Eat your heart out Arsene Wenger."
Christopher Davies, Football Writers Association Book Reviews, footballwriters.co.uk

"The wonderful book *Got, Not Got* – more of the same can be found on their equally superb blog."
ThreeMatchBan.com

"It is far more enjoyable to think about football in times past, and it is a seam that is
tapped so richly by authors Derek Hammond and Gary Silke, who have written a wonderful
A to Z of lost football culture, treasure and pleasures."
The Blackpool Gazette

"A book exploring the lost culture of the game when pitches were mudbaths, managers wore
sheepskin coats and players were too embarrassed to dive - a bygone age that seems a far cry
from the profit-driven game today played in the main by overpaid primadonnas."
Paul Suart, *Birmingham Evening Mail*

"Kampprogrammer, fotballfrimarker, fotboltegneseriert... smakfullt illustrert. Just get yourself one!"
PIN magazine, Norway

"This was in WSAG's Christmas stocking and it's fantastic.
Co-written by one of our fanzine chums Gary Silke, editor of The Fox, it is an amazing collection of
half-forgotten things and much loved memories. It covers mainly the 1970s when football itself seemed
more innocent (probably only because we were all still at school back then).
But if you're the same age as us then this book has your name all over it.
Admiral kits, football Action Men, League Ladders, Esso badges. On and on we could go...
Buy it. Well worth it."
When Skies Are Grey

"Outstanding."
Miniboro.com, the Middlesbrough FC, art and interviews website

"A great read with fantastic visuals, the book reflects on how football used to be before the sanitisation
of the Premier League. Amusing and quirky, this book captures the spirit of football from the terraces.
This book is an absolute must for any footballing household."
King of the Kippax

"*Got, Not Got* is wonderful. I'm feeling quite emotional leafing through it!"
Nick Alatti, The Bridge 102.5FM in the Black Country

"In an imaginary Victorian boozer in a sepia-tinted corner of the globe, old blokes gather to talk about
football back when it was good. It is a tempting retreat, with some fantastic flagship vehicles such as
Got, Not Got and 500 Reasons To Love Football using modern media to hark back to a glorious past."
theseventytwo.com

"It would have been easy to just produce a book of nostalgic memorabilia.
It's something else to have a book that captures the heart and soul of the time.
I didn't just look back fondly, I had flashbacks full of excitement!
A wonderful journey back into our childhoods..."
God, Charlton and Punk Rock blog

"A real treat – the ideal Christmas gift for anybody who loves their retro football.
With a page dedicated to Hull City, 'Fer Ark' and all, this is the perfect football book for this time of year."
Hull City FC official website

"Whatever the football fad that accompanied the era that you got into football, you'll find it all revisited in
the wonderful book *Got, Not Got*. It's a great book, every page has a throwback memory for any football fan
over 30 and you'll dip in and out of it for months on end as I have done."
Nick Sports Junkie blog